Mirror of Memories

Mary Jane Waynick

Mary Jane Waynick "2004"

Wasteland Press
Louisville, KY USA
www.wastelandpress.com

Mirror of Memories
by Mary Jane Waynick

ISBN: 1-932852-56-5

Printed in the U.S.A.

Table of Contents

ACKNOWLEDGMENTS

I hope that when you read this you will be inspired by my thoughts and through the Mirror of Memories that you will have lots of your own memories. That by reading this you may also write some of your memories so others may enjoy reading them as much as I have writing mine. That someday your children, grandchildren and others will have some mementos to remember you by. These are messages of inspiration, of love, hope, and healing. Messages that will comfort and relax everyone to know that we are all God's children. That he loves us all the same. I can say that I know this because he has helped me through all my trials and tribulations and he is there for us all. That God knows the heart of all of us even better than we know our self.

Thanks to all of my children for the inspiration I have had from them . Many thanks for all the others in my stories that have come into my life and have inspired me .

Thanks to the editors and those that have had any part in helping me accomplish my work for this book and in all their assistant that they have given me.

TO ALL MY DAUGHTER, MY HUSBAND AND EVERYONE THAT READS THIS

When you read this please have an open mind and remember I am not trying to preach to anyone. These thoughts are just a way of me expressing myself. I wanted each of you to have something from me and always remember how much love I have for each of you. Growth in the progression of each of us will come when we are ready. God has blessed me with a family that is loved and has given me love in return.

I feel that sometimes I have to be strong for all of you and for my grandchildren. But remember I am just as weak as each of you. Through my faith I ask for God's help to see me through the hard times also to take care of all of you.

No one church can fulfill everybody's needs at every level; there is no perfect religion for all of us, because we are all at different levels of spirituality. We should never criticize any church or faith, where people are seeking. God's religion is all about loving one another. I myself am guilty of criticism but I'm praying for God to help me over come my faults and make me a better person.

I want to write a little about each of you. Something special in my life. I can never write everything because my life is just too full.

Each person is different in personality, appearance, and talents, but you each have your own special ways. I hope and pray that you all know that you all are special to me, and that I love one of you as much as the other and I try to treat you all equally.

To my husband whom I love very much, even though sometimes I don't say it as much as I should you are always in my heart. I'm so thankful to you for all of my children and I know you feel the same way by me.

We have had some hard times but we made it and now we are suppose to be in our golden years. We still have our trials but with the Lord's help we still go forward, and I love you now as much or more than I ever did.

I have written a little about each of you, my daughters, I could just keep writing but just wanted each of you to have a memento of my love for you.

Chapter One

Memories of My Children

VELERA

My oldest daughter, I remember the day you were born , how scared I was because I didn't know what to expect. We lived in Tennessee on this big hill and it was two miles to a store and we had no car or phone. When I started having contractions your Dad had to go to the store to get someone to take me to the hospital. I had to stay there because the contractions were so bad. So we fixed a signal so if my pains got too bad he would rush back. We could see from our house almost to the store. So we hung a diaper up for a flag and if I took the flag down he would come back. Well poor Dad, I would have a contraction and I would take the flag down, then it would let up so I would hang the flag back up. I had him running back and forth. At the foot of the hill there was a house and the lady just happened to be a nurse, as he was on his way to the store she wasn't home, but he never found anyone at the store that could take me, so as he started back home she was there, so he asked her to take me to the hospital. We were just lucky to find her home. You were born about thirty minutes after we got to the hospital, which was about ten miles from our house. I was so scared and then, there you were that little bald head just shining, you were everything anyone could want.

Then when you started walking your hair was so pretty, with curls and one day you were going to fix it and you got the scissors and cut it so short I couldn't even fix it. I found all your little curls over behind the bed.

Then we bought you a cowgirl outfit and boots. You still wasn't potty trained so one day you wet them and put them in the oven. I turned it on and they were ruined. You just cried and tried to wear them anyway.

MY DAUGHTER'S ACCIDENT

My husband and I were on vacation in Tennessee. We owned a trailer there and we would go on vacation at least once or twice a year.

The morning on April the ninth, 1995 I had just gotten out of bed when my nephew came to the door and told me I had a phone call from Michigan, where we originally reside. It was one of my daughters calling. She told me my oldest daughter Velera had been in an automobile accident. She didn't tell us how bad it was but that we should come home immediately. It was about seven o'clock in the morning.

My husband, Eugene and I had to winterize the trailer because we didn't know when we would be able to go back to Tennessee. I guess it took us about three hour to get it done, and to get the car loaded. It is about a ten hour drive from where our trailer was to our home in Michigan..I think that is the longest ten hours that I can ever remember. You can never imagine what went through our minds in that ten hours.

We arrived in Michigan about nine that night, after stopping for gas and something to drink at the rest areas. When we got home one of our daughters was at our house. She told us Velera was in University Hospital in Ann Arbor, Michigan. That we should get up there as soon as possible because she was in critical condition, but that was all she could tell us. We still had about an hours drive to get to the hospital.

When we arrived at the hospital one of Velera's doctors met us and we went in another room and talked.

He told us not to be shocked at her appearance, but try to be prepared because she was in critical condition but they were doing everything they could possible do for her. The doctor went in the room with us to see her, and we were so shocked. We couldn't even tell it was her. They had to perform a tracheotomy, because she couldn't breath. They said they had to try several times before they could get the tube in. There were tubes in her head, throat, nose and mouth and monitors and IV's and everything on her. Also she was on a respirator. Her head was swollen twice it's normal size. She was also in a coma. The doctors said she had broken ribs and pelvic bone and her right side was bruised also her arms and legs. Her sinus cavities on her face were just crushed. Some of her teeth were knocked loose so the doctor had to pull them because she might get choked on them. The doctors couldn't tell all that was wrong with her until she got better. Filters were put in her groins to prevent blood clots. So now she has to go yearly to have those checked.

The accident happened around two-thirty or three o'clock on a Sunday morning. I was told and also by reading the police report that there were two girls beside Velera and a man in the car. They had been partying, the man was a designated driver. The accident happened at the intersection at Sterns and Deerfield road, near Deerfield, Michigan. The man that was driving was not drinking but he ran a stop sign and was hit by a pickup truck. The truck hit them on the driver's side. Velera was in the back seat behind the driver. The driver was killed. The two girls were not hurt real bad. One girl had a broken leg and was in a coma two weeks. The other girl had facial cuts and a separated shoulder. The one girl was taken to Bixby Hospital for treatment and released. The other girl was taken to Herrick Hospital in Tecumseh,

Michigan, where she was then taken to University Hospital in Ann Arbor, Michigan.

The Air Flight was called but they couldn't get to where they were because of the weather. So they did the next best thing, which was to go to Herrick and they were waiting for the ambulance so they could take Velera to University Hospital.

The police report said they had to use the jaws of life and cut off the top of the car that she was in to get her out. The man was pronounced dead so they took him to Bixby Morgue in Adrian. I have never got to talk to the man's parents, but I sure would like too. I feel so bad for them.

When we arrived at the hospital all of Velera's children and her sisters were there ,except the one that was at my house and she went with us up there. Velera stayed in ICU about three weeks, then we had her transferred to St Joseph Hospital in Ann Arbor. There my husband and I had several meetings with her doctors and the staff to discuss her condition and the different levels of a coma. Her children and her sisters were suppose to meet with them also. But her children didn't. I guess they thought I could take care of everything or they just couldn't stand to see their mother that way. I know it was very hard on them, but I tried to explain that it was hard on me too, and that their mother needed them. I talked to them and made a chart for one of us to be there everyday because the doctors said she needed us. That didn't work out so I went myself. I would get so emotional that I would have to leave the room because I didn't want her to know I was upset. The doctors said she could probably hear us even if she couldn't respond. They said that the hearing was the last thing to leave a person. So I sat and read to her and talked until I would have to leave the room for awhile then I would go back.

No one will ever understand just how hard it is to see one of your children like that unless they have had the same thing happen to them. I had to make some decisions that I never thought I would have to do. I was asked if I wanted her put on life support and if her heart stopped did I want her revived. I didn't think she would want to be on life support but I did want everything done that they could.

She progressed to another level of the coma where she would move a little if you shook her and try to open her eyes. The nurses would pick her up and tie her in a wheel chair and then tie her hands. They tried to get her to eat but no success. At that time she had a feeding tube in her stomach so that she could get some nourishment, also IV's for fluids and medication.

After she got so she would open her eyes a little we had her transferred to Special Tree in Romalus, Michigan. By then she was in another level of the coma. We still had to keep shaking and talking to her to get any response. When she had an appointment with Dr. Owen Perlman, her neurologist I would be there. They were still putting her in a wheel chair and had a tray that fit on it so she couldn't fall or get out. But still had to tie her hands because she was always pulling her trachea out. Then they would have to rush her back to St Joseph Hospital to have them put it back in so she could breath. She kept having a rash and it got so bad she was turning blue. I kept telling them that she was allergic to metal, but they wouldn't listen to me. Finally one day they thought maybe I was right so they took her back to the hospital and replaced the trachea with a plastic one. Then the rash cleared up and there wasn't anymore problems with that.

Then one day I kept talking to her and she was very agitated and she said mama. I was so excited and happy that I wanted to take her and hold her like I did when she was a baby. I just knew she was getting better. Also when she would get upset she said Candie, that was one of her daughters names.

One day when I went to the doctor with them, one of the girls on staff was pushing Velera in the wheel chair and Velera was dragging her right leg, which was injured in the accident, the girl got angry at her and jerked the wheel chair and caught Velera's foot under the foot rest and screamed at her. Velera didn't even know what was wrong. I told the girl that I never wanted that to happen again. Then when I got home I called and reported her to the supervisor. They either discharged her or transferred her one because that is the last time I saw her.

Velera finally got so she could sit in the wheel chair and push it with her feet as if she was walking and the nurses got her to eat a little. They started giving her more extensive therapy trying to get her right arm working again. I know it was so painful, because I went with her to therapy and I would almost cry myself. They said if they didn't do that , her right side might always be stiff and she might not be able to use it again.

After she started eating more and was more alert we transferred her to Tyler House II. We would try to keep her awake as much as possible when we were there. We would get her up and hold her and make her walk until she was tired. We saw some improvement, but then she became more agitated every time someone came near her especially a man person, so then we transferred her to Thompson House in Jackson, Michigan.

When she was in Thompson House they started doing more therapy and a one on one basis, and she still was very angry. So the staff took her to the doctor and he determined that she had Trichomonas. It had to have happened when she was in Tyler House II because it was right after she was transferred to Thompson House and had never been in contact ,only with the staff.

I contacted three different attorneys and they told me after doing research and talking to the staff at Tyler House II that they still could not get enough evidence for a case.. So I was really upset to think that someone could take advantage of anyone in that condition. That did set her back some because she had lost her trust in people.

It was in December 1996 that she was transferred to Thompson House. After she regained confidence in the staff she began to improve again. Velera still had the feeding tube in her stomach but by then she was feeding herself. So the staff asked me why she still had it in I told them I didn't really know, so they took her to the doctor and he removed it. The doctor said there was no reason why she should have it if she was eating good. When he removed it he left a piece in her stomach so they had to take her back to have that out because it was getting infected.

After that she started taking her baths by herself. She still had to be told and they had to show her how.

When she was still at University Hospital I had a

good friend from church to give her a blessing. He said she was so bad he couldn't even lay his hands on her head because she had all of those tubes on her. But with the Lord's will and lots of prayers she could get better. I prayed from the time I got the phone call in Tennessee all the way home, and I'm still praying. All the people in my church prayed for her. No one will ever know just how much I appreciate their prayers and all the help I've had.

Before her accident she loved doing crafts, painting, ceramics, and crocheting and all kinds of work with her hands. She had a computer and kept her finances and everything in it, and all kind of games. Also she had a full time job at M&S Manufacturing at Hudson, Michigan, working ten to twelve hours a day. Velera was forty- seven years old at the time of the accident. She has four children, ten grandchildren, and had five sisters but one of her sisters died in 1999 with lung cancer. She was next to Velera in age. They were very close and Velera had a hard time accepting her death.

The first of February 1995 just before her accident her husband, Gary died with a heart attack. She never really had time to grieve. I often mention his name, and at first I get a puzzled look and then I ask her some questions about him and she seems to remember or at least some recollection. Then she looks as if she is going to cry. They have to put drops in her eyes because she doesn't have any tears. I just tell her everything is alright. One time though she did ask why didn't he come to see her. If you are around her a lot you can figure out what she is trying to say. So I tried to explain to her that he had the heart attack and died, but if he could he would come to see her.

After Gary died she came to me and her dad and ask us if we would take care of her finances if anything happened to her. Her dad and I thought she should get someone younger, and we suggested her children. She said she that she couldn't trust them because she was afraid it would cause to much conflict between them. We never thought that something like this would happen. I guess we all just want to think the best. We told her we would. So she went to M&S where she worked and had me made beneficiary of her life insurance and her 401K. The children was willing for me to do it because she had told them that was what she wanted.

Then after I started receiving her money from the car insurance and from her work ,her children thought I had gotten her life insurance . I tried to explain to them that I didn't get that insurance because that was only at her death. I tried to tell them everything I did with her money and that I was doing it first for their Mom and if she died it would be for their benefit. I had a hard time trying to get them to realize it at first. Because they kept questioning me about everything I did. Then I would get upset ,because I thought that them being my grandchildren that they should trust me more than that. I told them they were my grandchildren and I loved them and I would do all that I could to help them. I told them I was buying CD's with all except what I was using for their mom benefit. They never did realize that until I got Scott Michener their Brother-In-Law, to do the accounting and he told them. Scott is Velera's Son-In-Law.

Eugene tried to tell them that I was doing what Velera wanted and that they should appreciate me more and not to keep calling and getting me upset. Also told them if they couldn't say anything nice to not call me.

I have her funeral expenses, the plot also the vault paid for. I had it fixed so if her children want to change anything they can do so.

She has come so far since the accident. She takes her bath, does laundry and vacuums and dishes and sometimes helps the staff cook. She picks her own clothes out when we go shopping and the movies that she wants to see.

My husband and I go to see her every Sunday if the weather is not to bad, and then we go see her through the week. We take her out to eat and shopping and for a ride. She tells us what she wants to eat if she sees the picture. The only problem I have with her is telling her she can't have to many sweets. With the closed head injury we have to limit her eating because she wants to eat all time. She doesn't know when she is full.

I feel that we have lost the daughter we once had but she is coming back to us gradually. Yes, there has been heartaches and grieving though I never blamed the Lord, because I know that things happen that is beyond our control. I am just so thankful that we still have her and the Lord has given us the strength and courage to go forward so we can still care for her.

The staff at Thompson House has a Christmas party ever year for their clients and their families. Velera's children usually go to something like that, but this year 2002 none of them came. There was only one of her sisters, Judy and her husband Steve that came, besides me and her Dad. I think she is beginning to realize more all time, she just can't talk and tell us what's wrong. Judy asked her what was wrong and she just shook her head.

Then Judy asked her if she was depressed and she said ,yes. I just wish her children could be more considerate of her feelings. I know they love her but it seems they just don't have time or won't take time for her. Meronica her oldest daughter, the one that is married to Scott does more for her than the others.

Christmas of 2002 has just passed and Meronica, picked Velera up and she stayed at her house for Christmas and then we all had dinner at my house and exchanged gifts. I usually have her with me at Christmas but this year she stayed at Meronica's. I don't think they have been to see her but maybe twice this year. My heart just aches for her because she acts like a little kid when she sees them walk in. She does me and her Dad the same way.

She seem to be improving all the time. She is really alert and hears everything you say. Then you have to explain what you are talking about or she thinks you are talking about her or it's something you don't want her to hear.

When I take her out to eat or shopping or for a ride we sing together. She does pretty good with the tunes.

I want to thank my husband, my children, all my attorneys and all of her doctors and all the other people for their support they have given me. The members of my church, because every Sunday I would cry. I felt that I had to be strong for all my family and my grandchildren so when I went to church I could let my feelings show.

Most of all, my love and gratitude for my youngest granddaughter, Rylie, whom I baby sat for when Velera was in her accident. I took her to the doctors, attorneys, and all the meetings we had. I think by me baby sitting it helped me to cope more with Velera's condition because I had to focus more on taking care of Rylie than feeling sorry for myself.

I also want to thank Judge Charles William Jameson for encouraging me to write this. Many thanks to everyone.

MEMORIES

It has been a while since I have written anything for my book. Though I have already written, and made a book for each of my children. I still have so many more memories that I think I need to share so I am going to start this and as I get the time and feel the promptness to continue I will keep adding to it. Sometimes we feel the need to express our self and the best way I know is to write, put it on paper so we can see it. My daughter, Velera just called me from the group home, she just wanted to talk. We don't stay on the phone long because I can't understand what she wants. But she has got so she calls me quite often. The staff where she is at in the group home can understand her more because they are with her every day. They tell me if she needs something or just wants to call. It is just a one way conversation, but she just wants to say hi and hear my voice. I hurt so bad for her sometimes because she tries so hard to talk. She can put some sentences together but not enough to hold a conservation on the phone. Since her accident in April, 1995, she has progressed more than any of her doctors ever thought she would, because of the extensive brain damage. They never thought that she would ever walk or talk at all or even remember any of us. We still don't know just how much she remembers, but I know she does remember some things. I don't think she remembers anything about the accident, because I have asked her several times and she just looks at me. Maybe it is the best that she doesn't. If I was younger so I could take her and care for her I would be glad too, but I know she is being cared for because her dad and I go ever week to see her. She is so happy every time we go. She is just like a little kid when she sees us. She gets so excited and is always ready to go out shopping and to get something to eat. That is the only problem we have with her, because of the head injury she doesn't know when she has eaten and never gets full. I always try and get her something sweet, especially something chocolate. Because that is her favorite.

Her neurologist calls her his star patient because she has come out of her accident so much. He never thought she would.

For a long time I couldn't cry in front of my children or grandchildren, I thought I had to be strong for them. It was like I was caring a heavy load on my shoulders. Then when I would go to church, ever Sunday the tears would just flow. I knew that my friends in church cared and knew what I was going through. I just felt more comfortable crying in front of them. Because I was always taught that crying showed weakness. That is something that my church has taught me, it is showing compassion and love not weakness if you cry, and it is a way of healing and grieving. Grieving is something that all of us have to do to heal our self.

Velera has four children, three girls and one boy. They don't go visit her very often. I don't know if it is just too hard for them to see their mother like that or if they just don't take the time to go. I try to tell them that it would mean so much to her if they would go. She knows them and is always happy to see them. She gets so excited, I know that she is happy to see them. I just wish they could understand that she needs them. I guess though we all just have to hope and pray for the best. They are all in their thirty's, so I think it is time for them to grow up.

I remember the day she was born and when the

doctor first put her in my arms, I was only sixteen, but the love that I felt, can never be expressed, except that of another mother for her child. She was just as bald headed , as if it had been shaved. Then when I took her home and her grandmother saw her, the first thing she did was give her a nickname, Witisie. It wasn't because she was so little but I had little shoes on her and her legs looked like a match stick stuck in them shoes. Her dad and I laugh every time we think of that. She still goes by that nickname.

I have felt the same way about every one of my children. I don't think it would make any difference how many I had it would always be the same. Also even if I had adopted children I would feel that way. I can never understand how some of these mothers can hurt such a small, innocent, helpless thing as a little child.

Velera has had such a hard time all of her life. Her first husband drink a lot and never kept them a place to live or any food half of the time. She would call me sometimes at one or two o'clock in the morning. The babies didn't have any milk and they were crying. I lived about five miles from her, and I worked at a factory, but I would get up and take her and the babies something to eat and some milk. Then finally we had to move her in the house with us because her husband became so abusive, fighting her beside the mental abuse. Then after her third daughter was born she finally left him.

Then after sometime she met someone else and got married. She had a son by her second husband. He was a very good provider but was abusive too the children and finally he started going out on her, with another woman and that ended their marriage.

Well finally she met someone else and got married again. He was very good to her and the children also. When the children were all grown up and all of them had left home except her son, that is when another tragedy happened. Her third husband, Gary had a heart attack and died. On February fourth 1995.

Then on April 9th. 1995 she had her automobile accident. She has closed head injury and has been in a group home ever since. She never even had time to grieve for her husband and now she just doesn't remember enough to live by herself.

I know it was just meant to happen that way but it is so hard to except sometimes, but with the Lord's help and his love He always sees us through our hard times.

She is such a loving person. She would do anything she could for anyone but she just had a hard life. But someday in eternity I know there is a better place for her. God always looks after us one way or another.

It's my prayer that some day her children and her grandchildren will visit her more often. She has ten grandchildren. They are from the age of seventeen to eight. So maybe someday they will realize just how much a mother's love means to a child.

KATHY

My second oldest daughter, I have written some about you farther on in my book. Kathy even though you have passed on to be with God you are still in our hearts. I will always remember the way you would hold on to my dress and follow me around. I couldn't go anywhere without you following. I use to sit at night and comb your hair it was so long. Then you would get tired of me combing and brushing it, so I had it cut short so you could take care of it. I remember the time you broke your arm and you tried to hide it from me, because you were wearing my high heel shoes, and you thought I would be mad. But it hurt so bad you had to tell me. We will always love you and thank God for letting us have you in our life.

There will always be an empty place in my heart, but Heavenly Father had other things in mind for you. So you are with him now and I know you are happy and no more pain.

ADDICTION

I remember when my daughter Kathy was so sick with cancer and in so much pain, that I felt so sorry for her. I tried to do everything I could for her, but it just wasn't enough. The Lord had other plans for her. One day she looked at me and said, " Mom you know that Velera is a lot better off than I am, because she isn't in any pain, if she is she doesn't realize it". I said to her, " Kathy someday we will all be where we will never have anymore pain or sickness". The Lord has certain things that each of us have to do while we are here on earth because we are now living in a probationary state and there is so many heartaches and pains we have to suffer before we go to be with him. All we can do is pray to the Lord to help us through them. Kathy was so scared before she died and I tried ever way I could to comfort her. She got to a point in her illness that she wanted me and all of her sister and her children to go out to eat every week just so we could be with her. So we set a date for Wednesdays and we would all try to go, at least some of us would and if we all couldn't go one Wednesday they would go the next. I know she said if she could she would have all of her family to move in with her, so we could be there all time. I tried to explain to her that we would all be together again some day. That we could be a family again. I told her that the Lord loves each of us the same. I know that sometimes we do thing that doesn't please him, but he is always very loving and forgiving, if we only ask him for forgiveness. But He does want us to ask.

Velera is the oldest of my six daughters. She was almost forty -seven when she had her automobile accident on Apri1 9th 1995. Before the accident her husband Gary had a heart attack the first of February and passed away.

So she just never had time to grieve, before she was struck with this awful tragedy.

After his death she came to me and her dad and ask us to take care of her financial affairs. So we agreed to, but asked her why she didn't get one of her children because they were all grown. She told us she thought it would cause to much conflict between them. So it really has been a chore. I never realized just what kind of decisions that I would have to make. That is in my other story about her accident.

I wrote a little about each of my children, so they could have something to remember me by. I know they could remember me anyway, but when Kathy became so sick with lung cancer I wrote her a letter to express to her just how much she meant to me. So after that I wrote all my other children a letter.

Kathy is my next oldest, she was born on October 5th 1950, and she passed away on August 20th 1999. No one can imagine how it hurts to have one of your children die, unless it has happened to them.

I want to tell you a little about some of my memories. Kathy was sixteen years old when she got married, to Tommy Brown andthey had two children, Dawn and Mikie When Mikie was about two years old, their dad was killed in an automobile accident. That was devastating to all of us. It was almost like losing one of my own children.

After Tommy's death, their dad, I took care of Dawn and Mikie for awhile. We went to the funeral home for the viewing and the children stayed at Tommy's brother with a sitter. I tried to get Kathy to let me take them to the funeral home but she just wouldn't hear of it. So after I went home with the children, Dawn was very angry. I tried to talk to her and she asked me why I didn't let her go see her dad. I explained to her that her mom was the one that said she couldn't go. Well, for a long time she was angry with me.

After that Kathy started using drugs. At first it was pills for depression, then it got a little stronger and stronger. I was babysitting for her some, but she had her own house so I wasn't with her all time, so I never knew at first that she was taking anything so strong. Then it got so bad that she was borrowing money from everyone that she could. Finally she couldn't borrow any more. She had borrowed my car one night before I knew what was going on, and she was suppose to have it back so I could go to work the next morning, and she wasn't back so I called her house and at that time her sister Judy and her Aunt Linda was staying with her. Dawn answered the phone and I asked her where her mom was, she said she didn't know. I asked her who was watching her and she said Skinny a boy that her mom knew. Then I asked about Judy and Linda and she said she thought they were in the basement. I told her to go look, and she said she wasn't allowed to go in the basement. So I said, where are you now, and she told me that Skinny had put them in the bedroom and told them not to come out. Her and Mikie, and Judy's and Lydia's two children were in there and they were crying. I finally got them to be quiet and told them to stay right where they were and I would be over to get them. I only lived about ten minutes away. So I called my-sister-in-law and had her to take me over there and asked her to watch my two youngest children that was still at home, and asked her if she would get them off to school. My other four children were already married. On the way over there we passed Kathy bringing my car home. I told my sister-in-law to keep going I wanted to find out what was going on over there..

When I got there Skinny and another boy was in the living room and I ask where Judy was, and they told me they didn't know. I asked what was going on that the children had to stay in the bedroom and why couldn't they go in the basement to see if Judy was there. I didn't get an answer, so I told them to leave and he said he didn't have to. , because he payed board. I told him that maybe I couldn't make him but I knew someone that could. So I went to the phone and he said they would leave because he didn't want to get Kathy in any trouble. He knew I was going to call the police.

I then went to the basement and Judy was there with a boy and I started hitting them and told them to get up stairs where they belonged with the children and I was hitting the boy and he was begging me to stop and he would leave. About that time Kathy came home . I was so upset that I couldn't drive so Kathy drove me to work.

I still didn't know that Kathy was on drugs. After I was at work awhile I had to call Kathy to come and pick me up because I was so upset I couldn't work. When I got back to her house I noticed that there was spoons on the stove that looked like they were burned. I asked her what was going on because I thought the children had been playing with the burners on the stove. So I got on to her about that and told her that the children was going to get burned up. I was very naive or you could say not knowledgeable on anything about drugs. Then she asked me to watch the children while she went to the store.

While she was gone I went to the basement and there was syringes and needles every where. That is when I thought that there was something going on. So when she came back from the store I confronted her and she denied anything like that. She said that one of the boys that was boarding there was a diabetic and the syringes were his. I knew better but I just let it drop until I could find out more. Because I knew that it was not sanitary, and if he was a diabetic that he would know better than to leave his needles and syringes laying around.

About the next day I had a phone call from Kathy's deceased husband's sister-in-law saying that Kathy had committed herself to a hospital. Then she goes on to tell me that Kathy had a nervous breakdown. Right then I started asking questions about where she was and why wasn't I called before now. Her sister-in-law said she didn't want to worry me. I said why not, " I have her children and I should be one of the first people to know." Then I became angry, because her husband and her was the ones to get her started on nerve pills. After Kathy's husband got killed, before the funeral they started giving her pills. I told them then that she needed to face his death and start grieving. Yes, it is hard but the sooner she dealt with the situation the better off she would be. So I told her to tell me where Kathy was and she said Mercy Wood, which is a rehabilitation center. I told her not to think that I was so stupid I didn't know what was wrong. Then she said, yes Kathy was taking heron, and she tried to take her own life so they talked her into committing herself.

I think it was about two weeks before we were allowed to see her. It was at Christmas time so we went to see her and at that time she still didn't know that we knew what was wrong. We talked to the doctors and the nurses and they told us that she wanted to see her children, and if we want to take her home for Christmas Day we could but no way let her out of our sight. They said she wasn't cured yet and that if we let her out by herself that she would try to get more drugs. They wanted us to have her back at eight o'clock that night for a treatment.

As soon as we got her home she got on the phone and called her other sister-in-law and wanted her and her husband to come over. So they came over to the house. When it was almost time for her to go back to the hospital she started telling me that her sister-in-law would take her back. I said, " no, I will take you." Then she started making excuses that I had cooked all day and it would give me a break. So I just said, " I am taking you and if they want to go with me they are welcome. But I picked you up and I will take you back."

When we got there each one of us could go up and talk to her for awhile. So first Mary's husband went in and we talked to Mary while he was visiting with Kathy. We told her that we knew why she was there and we would do all we could to help her. Then when Mary went in to see her she told Kathy we knew why she was in there. Then she started crying and Mary came out and they told me and her dad to go in together. When we did she was still crying and we talked to her and told her we wanted to help her, if she would straighten up and try to do better for herself and for her children. She said that was what she wanted to do, but she thought we wouldn't have anything more to do with her. It took a while for her to stay in the hospital, but when she was cured, she came home and then she made a home for herself and her children. Of course there is no complete cure because if she was to take drugs anymore at all, she would be right back on them.

The doctors and nurses told her to never take anything or she would be back there in the hospital again. I think she realized just what she was losing so she went to work and finally got married again and had another baby, by her second husband. He helped her to recuperate and she was fine then. As far as I know she never did take anymore drugs. She said that she was lucky and tried to tell everyone not to do drugs that it would ruin your life. In the back of our mind there was always that fear that she just might take something again. But all we could do was trust her and pray, that with the Lord's help she would stay clean of drugs.

She said, " thank you mom and dad for the support you gave me. I just felt that I had really messed my life up, and I didn't know what to do,. I felt that if you knew you wouldn't want to have anything to do with me. That my life would be over".

Then when she got cancer in 1998 , that was an awful ordeal for her and for all of us. She suffered so much. I never want to see anyone suffer that way and when it is your child it is almost unbearable. I know though that it was the Lord's will and with his help he saw us through it. It still hurts and there will always be a void in our lives. But we have to go forward and just hope that nothing else like that ever happens again.

Kathy was such a sweet baby, and always so close to me. She would follow after me and hang on to my dress and never want anyone else to hold her. When I started having contractions before she was born, I got my husband's brother to take me to the hospital. We lived about six miles from the hospital, but I had never been there to see where it was. So we started out and I was having contractions about three minutes apart, and we got lost. We drove about four hours before we could find the hospital. My husband, was at work. We left the house about eleven o'clock in the morning and we didn't get to the hospital until a little after three. Kathy was born about four thirty, so by then my husband was there. She was a very happy baby just as long as she was by my side.

When she was forty-nine and went in the hospital, that is when they determined she has cancer, she still wanted me by her side. They did surgery and removed her right lung but then the cancer spread to her brain. I stayed in the hospital with her. By then she had gotten married again to her third husband and he didn't want to stay with her. I can't really say she got much empathy from him, but I guess he was dealing with it the best he knew how. She was fighting so hard after her surgery they had started giving her morphine drip because she was in so much pain. Her dad and I was sitting with her and I told the nurse that she wasn't ready to die. I said," can't you see how hard she is fighting". It was a male nurse. So he went and called her doctor and they took the drip away from her. The nurse told us what ever we did to not leave her alone. So that night her sister and I stayed in the hospital with her, then the next night I stayed with her and the nurse put a cot in her room for me to sleep. I sure didn't get much sleep though, because every time I dozed off she called me for a drink of water. She wasn't really thirsty though, she only wanted to make sure I was still there.

Just as soon as they took her off of the drip she started talking and asking questions. So after that second night she did get her husband to stay with her the third night and then they let her come home. By that time they had already taken ultra sounds and found the cancer had spread to her brain. So when she got home she still had to go in for chemotherapy. So her sisters, her children and I took turns taking her for her treatments.

Her and her husband had just retired from working at Mid Michigan and had bought a camp ground near the MIS race track in Brooklyn, Michigan. So he was busy taking care of that. She never did get to enjoy it after she retired. Sometimes we just feel that we can never enjoy ourselves, after we retire. But that is the Lord's will not ours.

After she knew she was dying and only had a while left, she ask her husband not to take her back to the hospital. She said, she just wanted to stay home to die. So he agreed to that. When she got so bad her sisters and her two daughter took care of her until finally they had to call hospice. They came in but her sisters and daughters was the ones that gave her , her medication, until she got so bad they had to give her the morphine drip again. Then hospice only stayed long enough to give her a bath and tell them what to do. Of course she was almost dead then. That is the hardest thing anyone can ever go through. Watching your children suffer and know there is nothing you can do is like having your hands tied. She lived about eight months after she came out of the hospital. Her children and her sister stayed with her after she got so bad, I think about six day, before she died. Then I came home to rest because the children kept on to me to go get some rest. The night I came home she passed on. I knew in my heart that as soon as I left she would. But I guess that is the way the Lord meant for it to be. I am just so thankful that we had more time with her and I could talk to her and let her know how much I cared. It seems that there is so much we would like to say that we never can say it, and after the death of a loved one we can think of everything we wished we had told them.

After her death and the death of our little boy, and the accident Velera had I just wonder what else I have to go through. It is a sad thing when you lose your children. I know though that there are more people that have went through more than I have. I just ask the Lord to help me be strong and get through all the trials that come my way. I don't know how I could make it without the Lord in my life.

After the incident with the drugs Kathy tried so hard to do the best she could. I don't see her children much now, but I think it is just so hard every time they see me, I just don't think they can accept it yet, even though it has been four years.

It is a sad thing when you lose your children. I often wonder why our children just can't at least out live the parents. Then I ask God to forgive me because he knows why things happen and it is not for us to question him. I just ask him to help me be strong and get through the trials that come my way. I know if I didn't have the Lord to help me through them, I don't know how I could make it. I don't know how long it was before I could stop crying. But I would always cry at church or when I was alone.

There is one thing I can say, the hurt and longing for our loved ones never goes away. But we have to remember them for their love and the good things in our life. I know that the Savior loves all of us and he helps the pain to not be so bad. Because I know he suffers for all of us every time we sin, and wants us to live better.

I am trying my best to remember that my children are really all of Heavenly Father's and he only gives them to us for awhile. I am really appreciative for the time I have them with me to care for and to love.

JUST A CLOSER WALK WITH THEE

Just before my daughter Kathy died with cancer, I wrote her a letter and told her just how much she meant to me.

When she was small just learning to walk she pulled at my dress and cried for attention, and when she got older she pulled at my heart. We had some hard times, but our children are the most precious things that God has given us.

As she progressed in her sickness she kept asking me questions about dying. Would she ever see us again. She was afraid to die, which I told her none of us wanted to die. We just never wanted to leave our family and friends, but God had given us a way where we could all be together again, in heaven as a family.

So I tried to explain the plan of salvation to her. I told her that through the death of Jesus Christ that he atoned for our sins and if we obeyed his commandments that we could all be together again in eternity and if we do that and live the way he would have us to that he is there for us.

She started reading some and praying a lot, and just before she died she seemed so much more at peace.

I think that losing one of your children is the most heart breaking thing that a parent can go through. I have lost two of my children and I am looking forward to being reunited with them in heaven.

I can just imagine what the Lord is feeling when

we are disobedient, and what he must have felt when he gave his son Jesus Christ so that we might have eternal life.

How much more can we ask for and why is it so hard for us to live the commandments, and the laws, and serve the Lord as he would have us to?

Job chapter 11: 13–19
If thou prepare thine heart, and stretch out thine hands toward him; if iniquity be in thine hand, put it far away, and let wickedness not dwell in thy tabernacles. (15) for then shall thou lift up thy face without spot; yea, thou shall be steadfast, and shall not fear; (16) because thou shall forget thy misery, and remember it as water that pass away; (17) and thine age shall be clear than the noon day; thou shall shine forth , thou shall be as the morning. (18) and thou shall be secure, because there is hope; yea, thou shall dig about thee, and thou shall take thy rest in safety. (19) Also thou shall lie down, and none shall make the afraid; yea, many shall make suit unto thee.

As we read the words of God , how can we not believe, and have peace and know that He loves us. That he is a just God and He wants us to come back to Him.

Yes, we all grieve for our love ones, because of our loss and our human nature. Although we are grieving the angels and God in heaven are rejoicing for the return of our loved ones. They will be learning and serving in the spirit world.

Eccl.–12: 7 then shall the dust return to the earth as it was, and the spirit unto God who gave it.

I Peter–CH.1-2 For as much then as Christ has suffered for us in the flesh, arm yourself likewise with the same mind: for he that has suffered in the flesh has ceased from sin: (2) for he no longer should live the rest of his time in the flesh to the lust of men, but to the will of God.

As President Joseph F. Smith pondered upon the writings of Peter and our Lord's visit to the spirit world he said in D&C 138- 7-8 For Christ also hath once suffered for sins, the just for the unjust, that He might bring us to God, being put to death in the flesh, but quickened by the spirit; (8) By which also he went and preached to the spirits in prison. Verse 17 – their sleeping dust was to be restored to its perfect frame, bone to his bone and the sinews and the flesh upon them, the spirit and the body to be reunited never again to be divided, that they might receive a fulness of joy.

Jesus said, " I am the way, the truth, and the life; no man cometh unto the Father but by me." In Matt. 11, 28–"Come unto me ,all ye that labor and are heavy laden and I will give you rest."

No matter how difficult life seems, people need to trust in Jesus. There are things in ones life that maybe we can't talk about to everyone. Maybe you have been abused or hurt by someone, but you don't want to tell everyone. We all have to have someone we can trust and who better to trust than our Savior. Just know that He loves you and is always there to listen.

When Christ was teaching in the temple courts the Scribes and the Pharisees tried to trap him in his words. They brought this woman unto him, who had committed adultery and said she should be stoned. He then got up and said, "he's that is without sin, let him be the first to cast a stone". So they all left. Jesus said, "neither do I condemn thee, arise go and sin no more."

Have you ever wondered where the man was, who committed adultery with her? No one mentioned him, not even Jesus, because He forgave him also. He forgives us all. And has given us a way to return to Heavenly Father. Third Article of Faith reads, we believe that through the atonement of Christ, all mankind, may be saved, by obedience to the laws and ordinances of the gospel.

I know that Kathy is at peace now with Heavenly Father. We still miss her, but I have a strong feeling that she is happy and doing the work the Lord wants her to do and that she is not suffering anymore. I still pray for her and her family and hope that some how she knows that, and that someday her family will accept the gospel.

Kathy came to me in a dream one night, after I had been praying for her and wanting to know if she was happy. She was singing, Just A Closer Walk With Thee. I am weak but thou art strong; Jesus keep me from all wrong, I'll be satisfied as long as I walk, Dear Lord, close to thee. Since I had that dream I have really felt good. I know that she is with Heavenly Father and she is happy. I am looking forward to seeing her again, when it is my time to be with her.

LETTER TO KATHY

My dear beloved daughter I write this so that you will remember that I will always love you, and that God loves you as he does all of his children. We are born here on this earth to do what ever the Lord wants us to, and when we have finished our mission He takes us back to Him.

We never know what our job is here, but when we return to him then we will know. When you get to heaven please say hello to Mom and Dad and Tommy and your Tom for me. Try to teach them that we are all good. Sometimes we go astray but God is always with us, as the story of the Footprints say, when you only saw one set of footprints God is carrying us.

I am so grateful that God has given us more time together. We don't realize how precious our family is until we almost lose one of them.

I just hope and pray that all my kids and grandkids can someday realize the love that the Lord has for us.

When you were a baby you would cling to my dress and step on my feet. Now that you are older you cling to my heart.

I thank Heavenly Father ever day for letting me have you, so I could care for you and love you as much as I have and always will.

So Honey don't worry about leaving us. Because God has given you a mission and someday we will all meet again in heaven and what a wonderful time that will be, when we're all together again with God.

I know maybe I could have done more for you, but we are all human and as long as we are here on earth we will all make mistakes.

I remember the time you broke your arm and tried to hide it from me because you knew you shouldn't have had my high heels on. Another time I was trying to get you and Velera home out of a storm and had you running back and forth, because a tree was falling and I didn't know which way to tell you to go,

I know there are lots of things I could have done but we only do what we think is right.

Kathy I pray that this letter will be uplifting and not depressing, because you have a special spirit and you are unique. Only God knows how you feel in your heart. Someday we will all get to live with God and be as a family when we are all united in heaven. All my love to a special daughter.

TOMMY

Though you are not with us anymore, you are always in our hearts and our minds. You was our only son, and our third child. I appreciate the time that we had you in our lives, but the Lord had something else in his mind for you and your sister Kathy. You were such a good baby, you never cried. You would get mad at your sisters because they would take your toys and you would chase them. You never walked before the Lord took you at the age of fifteen months, but you could catch your sister crawling. We miss you but I know you are in a good place with God. I am so happy to know that you are with him.

MY BABY TOMMY

I have still got four wonderful children, fifteen grand children and twenty great grand children and one great, great grand child and I am very thankful for all of them. I am so blessed to have such a big family. We all get together on the holidays and just any occasion that we can. Christmas is our most special day. The day we celebrate the Saviors birth.

My little boy, Tommy was my third child. At fifteen months old we lost him to whooping cough. He was my only son. He never even learned to walk before God called him home. He was the most wonderful baby anyone could ever want. The only time he cried was if he was hungry, and then he only cried a little. But he sure let his two older sisters know when he was mad at them. He could crawl almost as fast as they could walk. Before him and his two sisters took sick with the whooping cough , I had polio, and was in the hospital for ten days and at that time my husband took them to get their shots. He said he was the best baby he ever saw.

I remember when he was in the hospital, I went to see him and the nurses wouldn't let me or my husband in to see him. We could only look through the window. Then one morning real early we got a phone call from the hospital to come as soon as we could get there, because Tommy was having a convulsion and they had to perform a tracheotomy. When we arrived at the hospital Tommy had already turned blue, but after they performed the tracheotomy he came back to. Then they took him to his room and he turned his head toward the window and smiled at us. That was the last time we saw him alive. That night he passed on.

We took his body back to Tennessee to the Waynick Cemetery where my husband's people are buried. That was so hard to let go but the Lord was with us then also. It took us a very long time to heal, but no matter how long it took, our memories of him are always with us.

We try to go to Tennessee at least twice a year and always go to visit his grave. We have room for four more grave sites, right near his. We have been in Michigan so long though and our other children are here in Michigan so my husband and I will probably be buried here. My husband also has two brothers and his mother buried up here. It doesn't really make that much difference where we are buried, because our spirit is already in the spirit world and the grave is only a resting place for our bodies. Because I know that someday we will all be reunited. We didn't have our son with us as long as we did Kathy, but he is still in our heart. We will always cherish the memories of each of them and thank Heavenly Father for the time we had them in our life.

JUDY

You are my fourth child and my third daughter. I have also written a little about you farther over in my book. But I want you to know how much we love you and glad that you are in our lives. I don't even want to think of it, if we had not found you when you were lost. I remember we bought you a stuffed santa clause for Christmas and I don't know how many times I caught you trying to flush him down the toilet. You were also special to us, as all of my children are. You would always ask your Uncle Hubert to make you some dump dumps, which is dumplings , when he would baby sit with you. You were always my most opinionated child and very stubborn if you didn't get your way. But we still love you just as much.

THE INDEPENDENT CHILD

After Tommy died I had another girl, Judy. She was my most strong-willed. At nine months old she was walking and very independent. She still is, which is the one thing that I have to admire her for. She has three children which she has raised almost by herself. Because she got a divorce when they were young. She has really done a good job and never asks anyone for any help. She is very conservative and she has a very good job working at a lumber factory in the office, placing orders for building material and checking lumber. Her and her husband both work at the same place. She only got married again just before her sister, Kathy died. Her children were all grown by then. She wanted to go to Las Vegas to get married so her oldest daughter, Janie and Kathy and myself and my brother from Georgia went with them.

The man she is married to now is very good to her and her children. Her children are all grown up and one is married and the other two are going to college. They are working and paying their own way, or at least part of their way.

Her oldest daughter is from her first marriage, and she has two children of her own. Which is Judy's grandchildren. Her other two children are from her second marriage. She has a boy and a girl, Stone, her husband as of now has two boys by his first marriage. Judy and Stone didn't have any children together.

When Judy was at home we had a time keeping up with her. She was always on the go. Her Uncle Hubert gave her the nickname, Galavanter, because she was so hard to keep up with.

When she was in high school we also had a time with her. She was in the tenth grade and she got all A's in her subjects, but she just didn't want to go to school. She would go to school on the bus and then she would never go in the building or go in then leave. I got so I would take her to school and wait to see if she stayed, but I couldn't stay all day so she would wait until I left and come out. She was just a typical teenager. She would be with some more students that had also skipped. Finally the police caught them skipping and called us.
She missed the bus one day or so she said and went to a gas station and called me to see if I would pick her up. I told her to stay where she was and I would be right there. When I got there she was with her boy friend and he ask if she could go to his house for dinner. I just wondered why they couldn't have asked me before I drove up there to pick her up. So I told him no and told her to get in the car. At first she didn't so I reached over to grab her arm and her boy friend said, " don't you hit her". So I had a belt in the car and I jumped out with it and chased him through the gas station and told Judy to get in the car. We came on home but the next day it was the same thing. So I just had to keep taking her to school. At one time we had thought of putting her in a school for delinquent teens. But the authorities told us if there was any other way to not do that. Maybe we could just scare her by a threat. So we did that and it worked.. A while after that she met another boy and they started going together then she quit school. They were going to get married but she got pregnant and then everything changed. She was so heart broken but I told her if he cared enough he would do the right thing. So we had a tutor to come to our house and she finished the tenth grade. Then when she went to the

hospital for her baby to be born she wanted me to call the boy that was the baby's father. I did and he came right up to the hospital. As soon as she got out of the hospital they got married. But he never did give the baby his name. I guess that was just as well because they never did get along, so finally they got a divorce.

After that she was married again and had a boy and a girl. When the children were still young she got a divorce from their dad. They just couldn't get along either. I don't know what their problems were, because I always tried to never infer with their lives. I believed when they got married they were suppose to take care of their selves, and they didn't need me to meddle in their business.

She has done a very good job of taking care of herself and her children. I have always told her if she needs me I am here for her. If she wants to talk or needs anything else.

She has bought her own house and car and is very independent. I admire her for her courage to stand up for herself. I have also written some about her in my other book.. She, like all of my children are very precious. She has a nervous disorder with her neck where it jerks and she has to have shots in it ever now and then. The doctors told her if she didn't have them it could snap her neck and maybe paralyze her. She really has a struggle with that sometimes. I can imagine how she feels because I have the tremors of my head and hands. But we always hate to see one of our children have to suffer and struggle so hard. You never hear her complain though. She just keep thinking positive, that someday it will get better.

Her children have all moved out now and she calls

me to talk. She said she is very lonely but she knows that is for the best. We all have to learn to let go so that our children can grow up and be independent.

JUDY GOT LOST AT SCHOOL

When my daughter Judy was five years old and in kindergarten she didn't come home from school one day. She was suppose to be home for lunch, with her sisters, Velera and Kathy. But they couldn't find her so they came on home.

We lived in Detroit ,and at the back of our house there was a railroad track, and it was very busy. When they got home I called the school and some of the children said they thought they saw her walking toward the house, by herself. So we started looking for her, by the railroad tracks and the longer we looked the more scared I became. So when school was over at 3:30 she still didn't come home with her sisters. We were still looking and then I called the police.

You can't imagine what was going through my mind . Maybe she got hit by a train, or maybe someone had kid napped her or something.

The police came and took one of her picture with them and asked what kind of clothes she was wearing, and then they told us to stay by the phone in case someone called. I couldn't sit still so my children and a neighbor stayed there. My sister-in law, Minnie, and I went back up the railroad tracks on both sides. We were walking toward to the school, which was about five blocks. All the neighbors were helping us look for her by then.

I had called the school earlier and talked the principal and she talked to her teacher and the teacher said she wasn't feeling well so she had let her go home that her eyes were hurting. The teachers were not suppose to let the children go without calling first to see if anyone was home. That day I had stayed home from work but I know that she didn't call. Usually I work but for some reason I didn't go in that day.

Well the closer we got to the school the harder I was crying. Then I saw the police car in front of the school so I started running, and as I got closer there were two policemen coming out the door with Judy in between them, holding her hands and talking to her.

I was so relieved and upset that I started to yell at Judy. The policemen told me to listen first, so I got quieted down and grabbed Judy and hugged her.

The policemen said her teacher had put her in a room by herself and had forgotten about her. Judy's eyes were all red and swollen from crying.

I was so angry I started in the school house to talk to the teacher but the policemen told me to let them handle it. They said they were going in to talk to her. I don't know what happened after that but she wasn't Judy's teacher anymore.

JOYCE

My fourth daughter, everyone tells you that you are just like your mom. But don't believe them because you have your own unique personality. Before you started to school I was pregnant with my fifth daughter and at times I was real sick. I had to rest a lot and if anyone came to the door you told them they couldn't come in because your mom was sick. Then they would leave and come back later. I remember when we lived in Detroit, you were about four and you were running in the house I told you to stop or you were going yo fall. Then all at once you jumped on Dad's guitar case and said, " look Mom". About that time you fell and hit your head on the coffee table. We had to take you to the emergency room and they had to put stitches in, I think about five stitches. They asked me to hold you and when they put the needle in to deaden it I started to pass out, so they had to get Dad. When he came out he was as white as a sheet. He told them never to ask him to do that again.

You had the colic until you were nearly two years old. Aunt Minnie baby sit for you while I worked. I worked until twelve at night and she had to hold you and walk with you until I got home. Then I had too do the same the rest of the night. I would get so tired bouncing you on my knees that I would go to sleep. One night you got quiet and I fell asleep and almost dropped you. I grabbed you by the feet and just caught you before you hit the floor.

Then I remember you were riding your bike and feel and broke your leg and the neighbors tried to make you walk on it because they were afraid I was going to sue them ,because you were at their house. Then after you got your cast on I was trying to help you get up the steps and I had you put the crutches up first and I almost made you fall again. But we finally learned how to use them.

You are also very special to us. We have been blessed and we are so glad to have you in our lives. We love you very much.

COLIC BABY BLUES

I remember when Eugene was working two job at one time, he ask me to fix him some cheese sandwiches. I fixed him cheese in both lunches for about three days. We still laugh about that. I don't know why I did it, I was just not thinking. So he said about the third day he opened his lunch and just threw it. All the men at work really got a kick out of that.

There is so many things that I just didn't know when we first got married, but when you get a family it doesn't take you long to grow up. Also Eugene was only twenty and he had some growing to do. Even though he had been in the service, it is altogether different in married life. Well I finally grew up, but it sure took me a while. After Judy was born I went to work for General Motors in Detroit. I worked there for seven years. In the mean time I had another daughter, Joyce. That made my fifth child. She was born in 1957. I had a pretty hard time then, because she had the colic until she was almost two years old. The doctors thought they were going to have to do some kind of surgery on her, but she finally got okay after trying so many different kinds of medicine. I had my sister-in-law baby sitting for me and I worked nights. I would come home and she would be walking the floor with her and then I would take over. I would get so tired, I think I could sleep standing up. I would burp her and lay her on my lap and sometimes she would get quiet and I would fall asleep. One night I almost dropped her and before she hit the floor I grabbed her feet and pulled her up.

There was another time I had to grab her feet also. We were driving down Fort street in Detroit and, at that time we didn't have seat belts in the cars, so she was standing up in the front seat and as I started to make a turn, I had the windows down and I caught her by her feet and pulled her back in the car, just in time before she went out the window. I know that the Lord is always with me, because he had to help me take care of my children. I just didn't know that much about taking care of them myself. I thank Him for that with all my heart. I also thank the people that invented the seat belts, and car seats for the children.

Now Joyce is married and has two girls and two boys. Before she was married her and her sister Judy use to fight all time. Now they are the best of friends. They could argue with each other as much as they wanted, but if either one got in trouble they would always stand up for each other.

When we lived in Clinton, Michigan, Joyce was riding the bike at a neighbors house and she fell and broke her leg. The neighbors were so scared I would sue them that they tried to get her to walk on it. Which I would never do that because all the children were just playing together. After we took her to the hospital and they put a cast on it, the nurse was showing her how to use the crutches. Then when we got home I was trying to help her in the house and I had her put the crutches upon the step first and then try to get her in the house and almost made her fall again. My mother-in-law was there and she told her how to get in. She had used crutches before so she knew how to walk on them. Well, I guess that is another one of my stupid mistakes, and I sure did make a lot while I was trying to raise my children, and I still do. But that is life we live and learn.

One night I had Joyce baby sit for my two younger children and she had some friends over to stay the night. I suspected something was up, because she was too willing to baby sit. So I left the house and about an hour I slipped back home. Sure enough they had their boy friends over. I had left specific instructions that they were not suppose to have anyone else over while I was gone. When I walked in they sure was surprised. All of them were sitting there with their PJ on with a cigarette. I just looked at them and told the boys to leave and made the girls go get their clothes on. At first her girl friends wasn't going to do what I asked them too. Joyce just looked at them and said you have to do what mom says. Well I guess they didn't have a very good night, but it never did happen again. But she still is a very good daughter and I would never trade her for anyone else. I feel the same way about all my children.

I recall an incident when we lived in Clinton where these boys that were the same age of Judy and Joyce they would always fight Joyce. That day this boy give Joyce a nose bleed and Judy jumped on him. My husband saw Judy and told her to stop fighting. Fighting is one thing that we didn't want our children to do. Judy was still holding this boy down, and she said, " Please let me do this just this one time." After he saw what this boy had done to Joyce he said okay and just stood there and watched. Well, after she let the boy up they never fought or argue any more. They became good friend.

Joyce also is a very hard worker. Her and I cleaned houses for a long time and she would work like a man. She helped her dad dig a water line once, when her dad was sick. I have seen her clean the barn and horses stalls. That was so hard that it should have been work for a man but she was trying to help provide for her family. She has a better job now working as a mail carrier.

Her children are all grown up and her two girls are married and have children of their own. She has two granddaughters and two grandsons. One of her boys is still in high school. He is a senior. She is divorced from their father, but seem to be doing well.

I am just praying that her children will finally grow up so that she can start doing things for their self and she can be happy again and have the life that she deserves. She is going to have to let go as Judy has. Because they are all old enough to be on their own. I have told all of my children it is hard to let go but it is the best for them, also yourself.

When it comes to your children it is very hard to say no to them. But once they get of age we have to let them go. They have to grow up and learn to take responsibilities and deal with their own actions.

TAMMY

You being my fifth daughter I have some memories also about you. I became pregnant with you not too long after we moved here in Tecumseh, Michigan, from Chicago, Illinois. I didn't think I would have anymore children, because Joyce was past six years old. But here I was again. We lived on Rogers Highway at the time and there was a little dog that came to our house and we called him Schooner. I wouldn't feed him at first, but I just couldn't let anything go hungry. He had a sore foot. It looked like it had been caught in a trap, so I started doctoring it and by that time he was our dog.

When I came home from the hospital after you were born, Schooner met us at the back door and grabbed your blanket and pulled on it until I sat down and he saw you, then he was okay. He would always watch over you when I had you outside. I could go in the house for a drink or anything and I could trust him to watch you. He would chase all the other dogs away from you. I had to watch you after you started walking, because you would follow him everywhere. One day after we moved to Clinton, he went across this really busy street and you climbed the fence after him. I called you and you said "here me am", I was so scared because you had crossed that street.

You were always so fast I had to watch you all time. Another time you slipped out of the house and went next door to our neighbors and crawled in the bed with her baby. She had left the baby there while she went next door to a neighbors for coffee. When I found you, you had powdered that baby and yourself with baby powder, you were both white it is a miracle that neither one of you were strangled.

You were always making Connie cry, because you wanted to play Cowboys and Indians or some kind of boy games.

I remember once you were outside and Brian Cooley and you were spinning the bicycle wheel and you got your thumb caught in it. I think your thumb nail is still damaged from that.

MY TOMBOY

Tammy was my sixth child. She was born in September 1963, and by that time Joyce was in school. Joyce didn't want to leave me. I guess it was my fault because I told her when I was so sick that she was my little helper and I would miss her when she had to go to school. At the time I never thought that it would have so much effect on her. Well, we finally got through that with a lot of talking.

After Tammy was born they finally determined I had epilepsy. I had a real bad seizure when I was in the hospital after Tammy was born, which I had, had several before but they never determined why I was passing out until then. The nurses and doctors saw me and then they did test. They said the only thing that showed in the test though was that I had a nervous system. So the doctors prescribed dilantin and I was okay for a long while. It never did effect my work for a long while.

When I brought Tammy home from the hospital our little dog meet us at the door and he grabbed her blanket and would not let go until I sat down and let him see her. From that time on he would protect her from everything. I could go in the house for some water or something, only just in and right out and, Schooner, our dog would stay right by her. One day there was a big black dog started in our yard and he chased it away. I was watching out the window just to see what he would do. After the dog left he came back and laid down right by Tammy.

Tammy was very much a tomboy. She loved to play Cowboys and Indians. So her and her sister would always argue about that, because Connie was the one that liked to play house and with her dolls.

I recall one day Tammy was watching television and we heard her screaming help, " Batman is killing Robin". She scared all of us so bad , but we still had to laugh when we knew she was watching Batman. She was always doing things like that. Also she was always running off. So I would have to watch her real close. She didn't know any different. She would wander off to follow our dog. We lived on a real busy street and I was so scared she would get hit by a car. She was not hardly two years old but she could get away so fast.

I had the baby laying on my bed one day and she had gotten a butcher knife out of the kitchen drawer and she said she was going to cut that baby's legs off. I caught her just as she got to the bed and told her it would hurt the baby if she did that. She never did that again but I don't know if she realized what I was talking about.

Then as she got older she was always so protective over her sister. As I said before she was very much a tomboy. She always wanted to be a veterinarian when she was growing up. She had dogs and ponies and finally got a horse.

We didn't live on a farm or a place big enough for her to take care of them as she should, so we finally had to give her ponies away. They keep getting out of their fence and my husband could not catch them. They just wouldn't let him near them, so he would have to go to school and pick Tammy up so she could get them back in their fence, and sometimes he would have to call me at work and I would have to come home and catch them and then go back to work.

Then the horse that we bought was just a colt when we got it and something was wrong with it. It just never did grow like it should and one winter it slipped on the ice and we called the vet and he told us to have our son-in-laws to lift it up and get it in the barn. I don't know why the vet didn't try to get him up his self, but he said he wouldn't do it, and told us to get another vet. We did get another vet and he told us the horse was malnourished. After we told him what we fed it he looked in it's mouth and told us that it had to be that way when we bought it, because it's teeth didn't grow like they should have. He said we would have to put it to sleep. So we did and Tammy and I both cried all night. The vet said we could get our money back from the man we bought it from but we never did try.

Well Tammy never did become a vet, but she has started her own business training dogs. She does obedient and some protection training. She is doing very good with her business.

She did go to college for awhile and she was studying to be a physiologist. She was also working to help pay for her schooling. Her Dad and I just couldn't afford to pay for her college. I wish she could have finished but she just couldn't keep up her work and studies both. But she is doing well now and she likes what she is doing and that counts for a lot. As long as she is happy.

She is living about forty eight miles from us but we see her about ever other week. I like too get with my children and go out and hear of their accomplishments.

Tammy is very smart and business oriented. She knows how to manage. I just hope and pray that she will always be that way.

When she was small I would tell her to do something , or not to do what she was doing and she would just keep on until I had to spank her, then she would grab me around the legs and say, " Mom I love you". Sometimes I would have to turn my head so that she couldn't see me laugh. Then I would ask her why did she just keep on until I had to spank her. But she just hugged me all the more.

CONNIE

You are my sixth daughter, and youngest child. You were such a good baby, that I could feed you and put you in your crib, or put you in your walker and you were very content. You never did crawl. When you wanted to get some place it was in your walker and then you started picking the walker up and walking with it.

I remember the time you and your friends put on a show singing and dancing. I can remember you always wanted lacy and frilly clothes, and wanted Tammy to play house with you. But Tammy wanted to play boy games so you two would argue about what you were going to play. I can still see you in that pink dress with white polka dots.

When I took care of Mikie and Dawn you were upset because you thought I cared more for Dawn than I did you, but finally you grew out of that.

After you became older and started going out, you and I were still close. You were very considerate. You always told me when you would be home, and if you were going to be late you always called.

After you joined the church you wanted to go to Utah to live. One of the missionaries gave you the address of a friend that you could stay with. So I thought I would go with you and meet Tom Patterson's mother. So we packed your little car that you bought from dad and went out there. By the time we got there it wasn't like we thought it would be, so we both almost started crying. You were going to stay out there and I was going to take a plane back. But we both wound up coming back together. The tires on your car was bad and they wanted to sell us one for eighty dollars. I said no we would just trust in the Lord to keep us safe. So we made it home and you still drove on that tire for quite a while afterward.

After you were married the doctor had told you that you probably would never have any children .because you had endometriosis . But you wanted one so bad that one night you said Tommy, your brother that had passed away, came to you and told you he had a little spirit for you and just a while after that you became pregnant with a very sweet little girl. She was born in January 1995 and was a very healthy baby.

PASSIONATE CHILD

Now I will tell you a little about my seventh child. Which is another daughter, Connie. She was born 1965. She is my youngest. When Tammy and her played cowboys and Indians after awhile she would try to get Tammy to play dolls with her. Most of the time though she didn't want to.

Connie was a very good baby and I was so fortunate because I was sick a lot after she was born. She never did crawl. We had a walker for her and when she started to walk she would pick the walker up and walk with it. That way she thought she was holding on to something, so she would go every where. She was the one that always wanted to dress in frilly clothes and dance and sing. She would always want to put on shows for us. She is still very talented. Her one talent is making jingles. Every Christmas she always has a different one on her answering machine.

She also loves working with children. Once she worked in a day care center. Then she worked dispatching trucks. She is very organized. She worked for a doctor, as his receptionist and the doctor she was working for had to retire for health reasons. So she went to work for the Tecumseh schools as a lunch person, which consisted of helping the children get their coats and attire on for recess and supervising them on the play ground.

Before she worked for the school she had to have surgery on her esophagus. The doctor did laser surgery and he cut her lungs and she almost died. They said it was only minor surgery, but we kept waiting and waiting for the nurses to let us know when she came out of surgery, and after about five hours I told them I wanted to know something. Her husband had already asked them and they told him she was in recovery. So I asked them to let us see her because I had to go home and I wasn't leaving until I saw her. It was about one hundred and sixty or seventy miles from home, and I had to get home before too late. So they finally let me go in the recovery room and I told them to get her husband so he could come in with her. When her husband came in I left and came home. She was still complaining, saying something was wrong, so she finally got the doctor back into check her and he had to rush her in for emergency surgery. They called me just as I got home and told all the family to come back down there as soon as we could. She almost died. Right now she has terrible scars on her stomach and also her back. It took a long time for her to get well, but we thank God that she is still with us.

Finally after she started working for the school, she was trying to get this ten year old boy off of a girl that he was choking and he grabbed her arm and kept hitting it and pulling on it until it was damaged bad. Now she has Reflex Sympathetic Dystrophy / Complex Regional Pain Syndrome. The boy injured her left hand and wrist and she can't use it. That happened almost seven months ago and she still can't use it. Finally she did get the Workman Compensation Stewart of the Tecumseh schools to try and get her some help and therapy. But the doctors said the Workman Compensation Stewart waited to long that it might be permanently injured. She has been to five or six different doctors and now the man is apologizing for not getting it taken care of sooner. But the damage is done and the doctors don't think they can cure it.

I just hope and pray that nothing else happens.

Besides that, her husband had, had a heart attack and a stroke, just before she had her arm injured. She has a daughter that is eight years old and with her daughter's and her husband's help they sure do get along good.

Well she finally out grew all her frilly and lacy attractions, but she is still very conscious of her dressing and her appearance. She still loves to sing and I hope she may someday be where she can do something with her arm.

She is very talented in writing jingles and poems and maybe she can excel in that type of work.

I don't know yet what will happen with her arm. I think they want to do surgery now and try to cut the nerve that is causing her so much pain.

I just hope she can see how much she needs the Lord in her life. She has so much talent that I hate to see her have so many problems and not be where she can use them.

OUR TRIP TO UTAH

Connie joined the church before I did and at one time she wanted to go on a mission. She was going to Utah and stay with a friend of one of the missionaries until she could prepare for the mission and I was going to take a plane home. We didn't know the lady, but when we met her we became friends at the beginning. She lived alone her husband was deceased and her children were away from home. So when Connie decided to go out to Utah, I saw the opportunity to go with her to Salt Lake to visit the missionary's mother ,that baptized me. When we got to Provo where she lived, I asked Connie her address and she didn't even have it. She only had her phone number. But with the Lord's will we just happened to get off the expressway at a phone booth and the lady only lived about three blocks from where we got off. The lady was real nice and she fixed a place for me to stay until the next day or as long as I wanted to.

We drove through in Connie's car and we would drive all day and before it started to get dark we would begin looking for a motel. We would have dinner and then get a good nights sleep and start out again. I really enjoyed myself and also the time we had together. When we went to bed even the first night I think we both were almost crying. Connie said, " mom I don't think I can stay out here without you". I was suppose to get a plane back and she was going to stay. The next day when we called home she talked to her dad and he told her that her check came in the mail and he asked her if she wanted him to send it to her. Well she looked at me with tears in her eyes and I told her if she didn't want to stay she didn't have to. She said , "dad I'm not going to stay, what do you think my sisters will say, that I am a big baby ?" He told her to do what she felt like doing and not worry what anyone thought.

We stayed there ten days but I contacted that friend of mine and she wanted us to come and stay with her. They were so nice to us she had eight children and we felt more at home.

I got to do a lot of my genealogy while I was there. Frances, the lady that we stayed with after the first two night would take us to Salt Lake Genealogy library and help me with my names.

While I was doing my research I found that I had a cousin on my mother's side that lived in Salt Lake and France took me to visit him and he gave me a lot of names that he already had researched. He said he was wondering when someone in our family was going to start doing genealogy. So I was real excited to meet him.

Connie had a real good time with Frances' children. While they were at school she went with Frances and I to the Genealogy library. Salt Lake, Utah, is where they have a huge library and all of the census records. so we did a lot of research on my ancestors. Then when Frances' children got home from school we would go back to her house and fix supper and read or play games one. That is after they did their choirs. Their dad, worked a farm and was a school teacher. They had cows and the boys always helped him milk.

Frances and Ed had a schedule set for all their children. Every morning before breakfast they had prayer and would read scriptures. Each one would take turns reading and then discussing what they had read. Then on

Sunday after church, they all got together and told each other what was on their agenda for the whole week. They almost had to do that because they were all in sports and all kinds of activities, and some of them were to young to drive and they needed transportation to get there. If they were going to ride with some of their friends, their dad had to know who they were and what time they would be home. Of course the children thought he was strict, just as I did my parents when I was younger. But with all of the things that are happening in these days, we have to be protective. There is so much abuse and killings and raping going on now.

Connie and I stayed ten days in Salt Lake, and then we when we started home Frances went to the store with us and we bought some food so we wouldn't have to spend so much on the road and also we wouldn't have to stop so much. We went back to her house before we left and she fixed all kinds of things for us to have to eat. We then left to come back to Michigan, and stopped for gas and the man told us one of our tires were bad and we would never make it . I asked him how much he wanted for a tire and he wanted eighty dollars. At that time in Michigan I could have gotten one for twenty dollars. So I told him we would just trust that the Lord would keep us safe. We got home just fine and my daughter still didn't get a new tire for a long time after that. He knew we were from Michigan, so I think, he thought he had a quick sale. But every thing went just fine for us.

Well everyone was glad when we got home and they didn't tease Connie too much for coming back. I think they were glad she did.

Now that she is married and has a daughter of her

own I just pray she will get back to church and get Rylie, her daughter in church.

Chapter Two

Laugh, Cry, and Make a Home

THE BULL

When my husband and I lived in Tennessee, right after we got married, we lived on a big hill and at the foot of the hill was a big barn and a creek. In that barn they had a bull and every time I went to the store or over to (Eugene) my husband, mom's house I had to go by there. So before I got to close to the barn I would try and be real quiet. But some way or other as soon as I would get to the barn that old bull would run to the fence and start pawing and snorting. I just don't know how he knew I was there. Then I would start running and I had to run up another hill. I kept right on running though because I was so scared he might get out. So I felt if I could get up the other hill before he could get out I could at least run into the neighbor's house that was there.

There were more cows and horses in the field that we had to go through to get to the main road and I was also scared of those, but if you took a stick and yelled at them they would go away.

So one day my sister-in-law was going home with me and the horses started coming toward us. I told her that they wouldn't hurt us to just yell at them. Well we had a bucket in our hands and I guess they thought we were going to feed them. So they just kept coming and I ran off and left her and I jumped over the fence. Then here she comes right behind me. She said, I thought you said they wouldn't hurt you. I said, they want but I didn't tell you I was afraid of them anyway. So just as we got to the barn that old bull waited until we got right next to it and then he stared snorting and pawing again. He always knew when we were going pass the barn even though we were quiet. Then we had to run up the hill to my house until we got out of sight of the barn. I think that was the last time she went home with me unless Eugene was with us.

Also when I was about twelve years old dad would take us to pick blackberries and that was also in a field where there was a bull. He would always let me, mom and my brother pick the berries close to the fence. Dad said, as soon as you hear me yell jump over that fence and here he would come right behind us. It sure didn't take us long to get over that fence. I don't know why I was so scared of all animals, except pets. Such as dogs and cats, and all the others I was scared of. I was even scared of dogs unless they were our pets.

The same field that the bull was in was near the road that my brother and I had to go near too walk to school. It seem like the bull knew just what time we went to school and would be there waiting for us and pawing and snorting. It was always the same way when we came home from school. There was a church across the road, where we went to church so we started going around behind the church. But that old bull would know anyway and he would wait at the fence until he saw us come from behind the church.

It was about two miles to school and we had to walk every day, there and back. The bus would pass us and if there was enough room for us on the bus, the driver would stop and let us ride. If the weather was bad he would usually make room if we had to stand.

I still am so scared of bulls. I dream about them a lot and they are always chasing me. I don't know what the meaning of it could be. Now that I am older and have a family I still have dreams of bulls chasing me. We even rented this house and the neighbor had a dairy farm and there was a bull on the farm. One day he got out of his pen and we heard the neighbor yelling and told us to get the children in the house. Boy, it sure didn't take me long to get them in. The neighbor sure had a time getting him back in the pen. I remember the bull was real mean because he had to get a pitch fork to keep the bull away from him.

Every time I dream of a bull I wake up crying. You would think after all these years I would be over that. I think I was just so afraid when I was younger that I just can't seem to get over being scared.

THE DAY I WALKED HOME

One day after me and Eugene got married and we lived in Abiff, Tennessee he became sick and had to go to the hospital. He wasn't out of the army too long so I had to get the ambulance to take him to Nashville, Tennessee to the Veterans Hospital. We lived about forty-eight miles from the hospital. There were no buses that ran near our house. The closest one was five or six miles. I had to get the bus on 100 highway, or in Dickson, which was nine miles and they didn't run very often.

I went to see Eugene one day and had to walk to get the bus and then had to walk home, so I had to leave the hospital so I would have enough time to get home before dark. Well I didn't allow myself enough time to get there before dark and I was scared every time a car passed. We lived in the country, so every time I heard a car I would jump off the road into the bushes and lay down in a ditch. I didn't think I would ever get home. Then when I got within a mile of our house there were more houses so I felt real brave. Then a car stopped and I just kept walking. Then I heard some one calling my name and she asked if I wanted a ride. It was my neighbor. Boy, was I glad. She gave me a ride almost all the way home.

We lived by a railroad track so I told her I could walk on the tracks the rest of the way. Just as I got in about two city blocks from home I heard shouting and something that sounded like gun shots and men shouting. Then I got scared again because I couldn't figure out what it could be.

At the time we lived in the house with Eugene's mom and dad. Eugene and his dad gotinto an argument and Eugene slipped and fell, when he did that is when he started hurting in his side and I had to call the ambulance. He had kidney stones and a stone had lodged at the kidney duct and wouldn't pass. After he was in the hospital a while the doctors got it to pass and then he was okay.

After that incident his mom left with her children and went to Arkansas, to pick cotton. So while Eugene was in the hospital I was left with his dad. I didn't know where else to go.

My parents lived in Greenville, Tennessee, and I just didn't know what to do. My sister lived in Columbia, Tennessee. I was only fifteen at the time and I had never been alone or had to make any decisions. But like all teenagers I thought I knew everything until it come time for me to make a decision. But when we are put in that situation then we learn very fast. Sometimes we just have to learn the hard way.

The closer I got to home I knew what was happening. Eugene's dad had a friend with him and they were drinking and shooting firecrackers. I didn't say a word I just went in the house and got ready for bed. . I didn't know for sure what might happen because they were drinking and I hadn't been married long enough to know his dad that well

So I went to the kitchen and got a stick of stove wood and took it to bed with me. I don't know what I thought I could do with a stick of wood but I was going to try and protect myself if I had to.

That was in 1947. I was so scared but no one ever said a word to me. Then the next day I went to the store and called my girl friend that I went to school with and her mom asked me to come and stay with her until Eugene got out of the hospital.

After he came home from the hospital we got our own house. I didn't know at the time that his dad was going to be there, I thought I would just be alone.

I never did let my mom or dad know what was going on. I just felt that it was my business and I had to handle it myself. Because my dad had told me before I got married, if I made my bed hard just lay in it and not come running back to him. I guess I just had too much pride to let them know. Well it sure didn't take me long to learn, at least some things. I felt I needed someone to talk to and my girl friend's mom was always there. My dad was real good to us but he was firm in his belief. That once you married and left home you were on your own. I know I could have told him and he would have helped me, but they were so far away.

All I did that night was say my prayers and finally went to sleep. My Father-in-law and the guy that was with him finally left and went somewhere else.

We had a hard time back then but I think it has made me a stronger person. The Lord has always watched over me. Sometimes we may feel alone but we are not, because the Lord is always with us. That night was a good experience, because I have never put myself in that position again. I always made sure to get home before dark or have someone with me.

HARD TIMES

My first daughter, Velera was born in Tennessee and then we moved from there to Detroit, Michigan. My husband had been in the army and he worked in Michigan before he went to the war. He fought in world war two. He came home in 1946. When he got out of the army I meet him, before he was even home but a little while. I was only fifteen and he was twenty. Right away we started going together and then we got married in January of 1947. I had Velera in April 1948. We stayed in Tennessee for about six months. He couldn't get a job that was paying anything hardly , so he came to Michigan and then he sent for me and Velera after he got a job and got a place for us to stay. He worked at Hudson Motor car for about five years. By then we had the two oldest girls. He was also working at a small factory where they made car jacks and lawn mower parts.

I also got a job at the lawn mower factory, sharpening lawn mower blades. I became pregnant with our son and finally I had to quit. By then Eugene was laid off, and a little while after that he got laid off at Hudson Motor Car.

So he went to Dodge Main and got a job there .That was in the year1952 when our son was born. Then in 1953 I got polio and I was so fortunate that I wasn't paralyzed or anything. I had what they call Bulbar Polio. The kind that sometimes works on your brain. I was in the hospital only ten days, but I wasn't allowed to get up. I couldn't even go to the bathroom by myself. When I came home my little son was only fourteen months old. My husband would get him up before he would go to work and put him in the bed with me and then I could manage then if I didn't lift him. Then when he was fifteen months old he died with whooping cough.

My husband was laid off at Dodge Main then, and he had a job at another small factory. In 1952 I became pregnant with my fourth child. Eugene got laid off again and they didn't want to pay him his unemployment compensation. Which he could have drawn on Dodge Main and also the other place where he worked. So we had no other choice but go to try and get some assistance from the state. By then I was eight months pregnant with my fourth child. He told them that all he wanted was his compensation. I don't know how they did it but he started getting his checks. So we didn't have any insurance so I had to go to Receiving Hospital for Judy to be born. They only charged us forty-five dollars for delivery and everything.

Before they would give us any assistance at all they told Eugene for me to go to work. He said, " great, who do you think will hire her, will you give her a job?" So that settled that but we had to wait until he got his compensation before they did anything, they wouldn't even as much as give us groceries.

I can't understand how some people can get help so easy and the ones that really need it can't. I think the system really stinks. But with the Lord's help we made out just fine. We had friends and our faith to help us through. Then they finally got the unemployment office to release his checks.

WHEN THE FBI PICKED ME UP

I was working at General Motors, Fleetwood plant in Detroit, Michigan, on west Fort Street and West End. The year was 1956.

I had three children and I had lost a little boy at the age of fifteen months with Whooping Cough. My two oldest children was also in the hospital with it, but they had, their shots, so they were okay after awhile. One of them was hospitalized only three days and the other nine days. I brought Velera home on the third day and Kathy home on the nineth day. Then my little boy started having convulsions and we rushed back to the hospital but he passed away the next day. Then after that I became pregnant with Judy. She was about two years old and we lived on Vinewood Street.

One day we went to Tecumseh, Michigan, where my Mother-in-Law lived. We would go out to visit her because it was more in the country and there were rivers and lakes so we could go swimming and fishing. This particular week end we went fishing. Well we didn't catch any fish but sure did catch the bites from mosquitos. We spent the week end and came back home on a Sunday night so we could be ready for work. My husband and I both worked afternoons. That night before I went to bed I had to put calamine lotion all over me because I itched so bad.

Monday morning we were woke up by a knock on the door. My husband went to the door and then he called me and said there were two men that wanted to talk to me. I grabbed my robe and ran to the door. There were two men and they showed me their badge and said they were from the FBI. I couldn't imagine what they wanted, but they said they wanted to talk to me outside away from the children. I asked them to wait until I could get dressed and they said no just come out to the car and talk. I was so scared I didn't know what to do so I went out there. When I started to get in the back seat there was some brass knuckles laying on the floor and they grabbed my arm and pulled me back. They reached in and picked them up and said I don't think you need these back there. Well, I said " I don't guess I do, because I don't know what they are."

Then they got in the car and started it and I asked them what were they doing. They then handed me a pencil and paper and asked me to write on. I thought they said Mary and Dick so I started writing. They said write it ten times, then I handed it back and they were so mad. I asked them what was wrong they told me it was suppose to be a girls name. Well I didn't know that so they were mad and started pulling away from the curb. I was so scared and asked them what they were doing and then they told me I should know I was the one that forged the check. I said, "what check"? They just keep saying I should know. I asked them where they were going and kept pleading with them to let me get some clothes on. They still wouldn't, they said we were going out to where I worked so they could have someone identify me, and told me I wouldn't have to get out of the car.

We drove out to the plant and they went in a barber shop just across the street. One FBI man stayed in the car with me and the other one went in the barber shop. Then when he came out of the barber shop there was a man with them that I knew, because I worked with him. The one kept asking the man questions and the one that was with me told me to get out. I said, "you told me I wouldn't have to get out of the car". But he insisted. So I stepped out on to the sidewalk with my robe on and that calamine lotion all over me.

The man that the FBI man was talking to kept nodding his head, first yes then no. I said, " what is he saying"? They just kept saying, you should know you signed the check. I asked them what check they were talking about and they finally told me the one that belonged to Mary Ann Dick. I still was very much surprised. I just kept saying what check. They said an income tax return check. I told them I didn't know what they were talking about, and asked them how much was the check., but they kept trying to get me to confess. They finally told me the check was $142.00. I told them ever who said I did that just didn't know what they were talking about. They told me then that they had been watching me for eight months. They told me everywhere I went and who I was with and what jobs I did at work and who I was working by and everything. They said you went across the street at lunch and had drinks with that one man and another one. I told them I was over there but not with the men. I had went with some more girls and had lunch. Then I remembered them in the factory standing watching me, but I thought they were some of the men at General Motors just watching us work.

Finally the FBI man that was talking to the one from work, left him and came back to the car. I said, " what did he say"? Then they started in again saying I should know because I forged the check. Then I was so upset I was crying and trying to talk at the same time. I told them I had children and if I was going to forge anything it would have to be for more than a small check like, $142.00. I had more to think about than money.

Then they started the car and I asked them where were they taking me. They said again you should know if you signed the check.

So we were on our way to down town Detroit where the jail was, but it was also toward my house. Then we got to the street where I lived and they turned and told me they were taking me home, that the man told them that I wasn't the one that forged it. Then I really started crying I was so happy and mad at that man and also the FBI, I didn't know what to say. If I had known then, what I do now I would have had something done with the way that was handled.

When I got home before they let me out of the car they said not to say anything at work, about what had happened because it would just be embarrassing to me and that no one needed to know.

Well I went in the house and finally got ready for work and just as I walked up to the time clock the man that the FBI had talked to and his buddy met me there and tried to joke about it. They said I heard you got picked up by the FBI today just so everyone could hear them. I told them to get away from me and never come near me again. They said, " Mary we had to tell them it was you to keep someone else from getting in trouble". I said< " thanks for all the trouble you caused me just never speak to me again".

I never did hear anything more about, who forged it and I was so naive I just thought I had to do what ever the FBI wanted . I just wish I had known that I could have done something about the way they handled it.

I think that is why I am so distrustful about some things now. I guess we live and learn. Why can't we just learn sooner.

ON THE MOVE

When Joyce was three years old we moved to Chicago, Illinois. Eugene was laid off again and I was still working at General Motors in Detroit. So I took a leave from work and we both went to Chicago to look for work.

He got a job at General Motors in Chicago and I got one at Borden's Ice Cream. Boy, that was even worse than General Motors in Detroit. They had us working, packing ice cream so fast that I didn't have time to wipe my nose. That was really bad because I had a cold. So I quit that job and got one printing envelopes. I only made $1.25 an hour, but that was the best job I ever had. I was learning to set the print and they wanted me to stay. My husband got laid off at General Motors so we packed our things and moved back to Michigan. Because there was no way we could live on $1.25 an hour, with four children. We had only been up there eight months, so we figured if we needed help , we should have it coming from Michigan because that is where we had worked the most of our life. We had been in Michigan fourteen years, and only eight months in Illinois. So that is when we decided to come back to Michigan.

We came back to Tecumseh, and stayed with his mom for two weeks then we found an apartment. We started doing odd jobs and was making $100.00 a week, which was good money in 1962. We ask the farmers if we could pick up corn, that was, after they had already picked it with the corn picker. So we did good that summer. Before it started to get cold Eugene had already found him another job in a factory. He was arc welding. And then we had found a house to rent. The house needed a lot of work, such as painting and redecorating. So the landlord gave us three months rent if we did the work. I have never seen a house that dirty. I would clean awhile and then go out side and be sick. We were still living in the apartment until we could clean the house and get it ready to live in.

We would fix a sack lunch for all of us, take the children with us when we picked up corn. If they got tired we had a blanket so they would go under a tree where there was shade and play until we finished work.

After we moved into the house we still had a hard time getting use to living out in the country. We had always lived in town. So it was really hard for us to get use to the country. We were used to going to the store at all times, wether it was at night or just anytime. So we would forget to get milk or bread and the stores closed early. The old car we had didn't have very good tires so we were always fixing flats so Eugene could have a way to work. Sometimes while he was at work I would fix a flat so he wouldn't have to do that after he got home. We had some extra tires but still couldn't keep them fixed.

By that time I was pregnant again with my sixth child. Joyce wasn't old enough to go to school. I was pretty sick with that pregnancy and I had to rest a lot. Joyce would keep the doors locked and stay right by me while I would rest. If anyone came to the door she would tell them I was sick and they would have to come back another time. There was a hole in the door where a door knob was taken out, so she would look through that. I had told her never open the door for anyone so she wouldn't. Sometimes I think I depended on her too much to watch while I rested, but I would always give her something to do. She played with her dolls or other toys and then she would color. I would always tell her how good she was to help me. Even when Joyce was real small she would sit in the bed at night, if she couldn't sleep and play with her dolls, and let me sleep. I told her I thought she could see in the dark.

Even when she got old enough to baby sit she would take her money and buy things for us. She never thought about herself first. She would always ask us if we needed anything.

THE FIRST HOUSE MY HUSBAND AND I BOUGHT

We bought this old house and it needed a lot of work done on it. It was very reasonable, so we thought it was a good buy. There was a big barn right beside it. In fact all you had to do was walk out the door and right into the barn. I can't understand why anyone would build a barn that close. Anyway we had to have it torn down before we even moved in, because we couldn't get insurance until we did. Our landlord from the other place we lived had a bull dozer, so we got him to tear it down for us. Then he dug a huge hole and that is where we gathered all the wood up and burned it. My sister-in laws and brother-in-laws, and our children all pitched in and helped us to clean it up. It took a good two years and even after five years we still was picking wood up that had been buried in the ground from when the barn fell.

Before we moved in my girl friend and I had to clean it, before it was good enough to live in. The kitchen roof and ceiling had fallen in right on the table. The people that lived there before we bought it, it just looked like they got scared and ran. The table was still set and there was food on the plates. It was a mess. Faye, my girl friend helped me so much I will never be able to thank her enough. We had to haul water from the other house I lived in to wash all the walls and floors. There was four or five rugs on every floor and they had nails about two and a half to three inches long to hold them down. By the time we got the rugs all torn up and the floors scrubbed our knuckles were all bleeding.

Besides that it had five space heaters in it and neither one of those was any good. We had to have a new roof put on and the ceiling in the kitchen fixed, and had to buy a furnace before we could move in. From using the space heater the walls were all blackened. There was not one closet in the whole house and they had their clothes hung up on nails. Where the clothes were hung on the walls there was just the prints of them, it was so black. Also the colors of the paint where you could see it was pink and turquoise.

My husband and I did the work just as we got the money. We would fix one room at a time. There was three bedrooms, living room, kitchen and a bathroom. It sure took us a long time to get it fixed. We couldn't buy rugs at the time so Faye and I scrubbed the floors and just left them bare. They were these old big floor boards. It took us a while before we could afford even rugs, but at least it was clean.

Faye would come over to the house after we moved in and help me clean the yard and everything. She was a real true friend. I remember when we were having it so hard she gave me food and other stuff. I don't think anyone could have a better friend. I will never be able to repay her for what she has done for me.

When I first met Faye we lived in Clinton, Michigan. We were neighbors and every day we would get together and have coffee. That was before I stopped drinking coffee. Her children and mine were about the same age, only I had some older than hers. At that time I was working full time at a factory and I was very nervous, so I know I sure didn't have the patience with our children that she did. I look back now and wish I could have been as patience and caring as she was. She always had time for her children. They were her life. But also she had time for others that needed her.

Awhile after we had bought this old house Faye and her husband bought a house near Adrian. I guess it was about five miles from me, so we still visited often.

We only lived about four or five houses apart in Clinton. One day I started into town and as I backed out of my drive I hit her car. The people next door had some horse trailers parked by the roadside and part way in their yard and they were obstruction the right of way. But that still didn't give me any excuse I should have been more careful. Her mother and sister were in the car. Her mother was driving and when I hit the car I thought I had only hit a bump in the drive so I just kept going backward. Her sister said, " mom she is coming after us again". Well at the time it wasn't funny but after we thought about it, it sound funny. No one was hurt and I was so thankful for that. Then when she honked the car horn I looked back again and realized what I had done. We got everything all settled and I went on to town.

There is so many things that happened I will never forget. I am so glad we can over look our differences and still be friends.

Then we kindly got away from each other. She got married again and moved farther up north, to Mendon, Michigan and we sent cards to one another but didn't get to visit much. Of course by that time my children and also hers had grown up.

Then after my daughter died with cancer, her husband got sick and passed away and then she moved back closer to where I live. I haven't got to see her much because my husband has been sick and with the daughter I have in the group home it just seems to take all my time. I hope someday we can get to be with one another more often. It just seems that as we get older we can't keep in touch as much as we would like. In the summer we see more of each other. She is someone that a person will never forget. I hope that she knows just how much I appreciate her friendship and love. I am trying to be as kind as she is. I think of her and just hope she knows how much I care.

Since we have bought us a new house she still comes over and helps me clean. I hope that someday I will be where I can do as much for her as she has for me. If I never get to do that, maybe the Lord will bless her for someone else to do for her.

I have so many fond memories when we use to get together and just visit. I really do miss her now. But as the old saying goes life goes on. Sometimes it don't go like we wish but the Lord knows what's best. Doesn't make any difference how things go, she is the best friend I have.

A while after we moved here there was a house for sale just up the street from us. When it was sold I meet the people who bought it. Then we became good friends. The lady had two boys that were near my two youngest daughters age. She became another one of my favorite friends.

Every morning her boys would come down to my house and wait on the school bus with my daughters. They became so close they were almost like my grandchildren. They would come to my house and hide my cigarettes and make me so angry with them. I know

now they were only trying to do what was best for me. They wanted me to stop smoking, but at that time I just wasn't ready to stop. I really did think that they were just a little to forward, because they would go to the refrigerator and take them out. But it didn't make any difference how much I yelled at them, they would never get mad at me.

One day my grandchildren and her boys came to my house and they started throwing my peaches at the cars that were passing. I remember going to the shed and getting a fishing pole after them, of course I never did hit them, I just scared them into thinking I was going to. But they never did throw peaches at the cars anymore.

As the years went by Nancy, their mother and I became so close that she considered me as a second mother. She introduced my youngest daughter to the Latter Day Saint missionaries and she soon joined the church. So I wanted to find out about their faith and beliefs in God. Then one day as my daughter left her Book of Mormon laying on the table I started reading it. It was so interesting that I guess you can imagine what happened. So after I joined the church I have felt so much better. There is just so much we don't know unless we study our scriptures and live the commandments. Nancy never did pressure me into believing her way, she just supported me and was always there for me when I needed her. We had so many good times together, going to church and the church activities and shopping.

At that time I was having seizures. Sometimes I would have three or four a week and I had doctor appointments all time. They were trying to find something to control them. Besides I was working and would have a seizure at work and have to have someone bring me home and sometimes they would take me to the hospital from work.

Finally I had to go on disability and all that time Nancy would take me to the doctors and stay right with me. She would have to take me to Ann Arbor, Ypsilanti, and Detroit. I have been very fortunate to have two wonderful friends that helped me so much. Of course I have more than those two, but I just wanted to mention a little about them.

Then Nancy moved away into another town and for awhile I was lost again. We still keep in touch and we send e-mails to each other but it just isn't the same. But since my husband has been sick I have been staying close with him. The doctors finally got my seizures under control. I know that the Lord is watching over us because now I can be there for him when he needs me.

Chapter Three

Poems...Some Original, All Inspiring

MY GIFT

At the time I was born, God gave me a spirit
He trusted me to worship him, and always care for it.
For me to grow in love and health–
So someday I can live with him in all his wealth.
Always testify of His love–
And I will always soar high above,
To share with him, all his love,
And be with others in their despair,
Showing them that, they are also, in His care.

My gift is a treasure that I adore–
Sent from God above.
To nourish, to care for----
And to love,
To give him thanks for all his care,
For the great gift that Jesus Christ did bare.

His love for us , is beyond our wealth,
He gave us a body to care for it's health.
In our body our spirit dwells–
As a little seed it swells and swells.
To God my Father up above.
I'm forever grateful for his love.

By Mary J. Waynick

CHRISTMAS DAY IS NEAR

As Christmas Day is drawing near,
We find ourselves rushing ,
Almost in tears
Let's stop and think why–
We know that God is with us , if we try.

So dry those tears and rush no more,
God is with us , at everyone's door.
Just take a minute and say a prayer—
I've found that he is right there.

All the good food and all the gifts,
Is also made possible with God's help
Not our thrift.

It's a time to be happy and not rush,
God gave us Jesus on whom we can trust.

Remember it's Jesus' birth we celebrate.
Something that has been for year elaborate.

So say your prayers and be with– Him
And all the Christmas' is worth all your trim.

As He is with us today,
Let's do his will and pray.

By Mary J. Waynick

WHEN GOD CALLS

We are here but a short
While to do our deeds.
Then God calls us,
For his needs.

We want to hold on to–
The ones we love, for our self.
But we have to let go,
Because God needs us for
Himself.

We have to be strong and,
Go right on
Because God will soon–
Call us all to his throne.

Even though it hurts to,
Let go–
God always makes the Best choices
we know.

So let's pray together,
And do what is right,
And he will see us
Through the night.

Sometimes it is hard not
To question God
But he will always be with us,
his staff and his rod.

By Mary J. Waynick

ONE SOLITARY LIFE

He was born in an obscure village, the child of a Peasant woman.
He grew up in still another village where He worked in a carpenter shop until He was thirty.
Then for three years He was an itinerant preacher.
He never wrote a book.
He never held an office.
He didn't go to college.
He never visited a big city
He never traveled two hundred miles from the place where He was born.
He did none of the things one usually associates with greatness.
He had no credentials but himself.
He was only thirty-three when the tide of public Opinion turned against him.

His friends ran away.
He was turned over to his enemies and went through the mockery of a trial.
He was nailed to a cross between two thieves.

While He was dying, His executioners gambled for His clothing, the only property He had on earth.

When He was dead, He was laid in a borrowed grave through the pity of a friend.
Nineteen centuries have come and gone, and today He is the central figure of the human race and the Leader of mankind's progress.

All the armies that ever marched, all the navies that ever sailed, all the parliaments that ever sat, all the kings that

ever reigned put together have not affected the life of man
on earth as much as that
one solitary man.

Author Unknown

IN PRAISE OF MOTHER

It takes a while to realize
All the things a Mother will do
To guide and help her children
And make home life happy too...

It takes a lot of birthday cakes
And toys now laid aside
To know her love and trust in us
Are the things that still abide...

It takes many hours of teaching-
Of dividing right from wrong
To appreciate her wisdom
And her faith so deep and strong...

And after all the years in which
She's cared and helped and planned
She's rewarded when her children say,
"Now at last we understand."

Author Unknown

Chapter Four

Spirituality and Faith
"How We Live"

LOVE

Love is a beacon of hope in this world of disaster. Things are happening in this world that is very distressing. The war in Iraq that has gotten everyone nervous. There are loss of jobs, people are homeless and hungry. Sometimes we think that only the people in foreign countries are hungry, cold and no place to live, but that isn't all true . We have people here in America that need help. We are very fortunate to live in America, but we must try to help those, that we know that are in need.

There are also wars of different kinds. Drug wars, affliction of diseases, and misery from heartaches. We have modern medicine and the knowledge of our doctors to help us with our pain, but kind words and the love of our savior, and the love for one another can bring to pass miracles. We must all pray together and do everything that we can for our service men and women, and also our loved ones here at home.

We are blessed with the good things of the earth. We see it this time of year in the budding of the trees and the flowers, the perfuming of the air, the sun, the rain and all living things. The forest, the birds and their beautiful singing. The Robins that have come back since winter to build their nest and reproduce.

Everything we have reflects the love of our savior, Jesus Christ and shows us how much he loves us. He is all around us. We may not see him but we can see his love. Sometimes we can even feel his touch, his hand on our shoulder guiding us.

As we look around at all the little children we

think of the disciples saying unto our Savior, "Who is the greatest in the kingdom of heaven"? And Jesus called a little child unto him and set him in the midst of them. "And said verily , verily I say unto you, except you be converted and become as little children, ye shall not enter into the kingdom of heaven." "And whoso shall receive one such little child in my name receiveth me." "But whoso shall offend one of these little ones which believe in me, it were better for hin that a millstone were hanged about his neck, and that he were drowned in the depth of the sea. MATT. 18: 1-6.

Little children are so precious to us, they are so innocent and caring and trusting. They teach us the love of Christ so we must teach them the principles of the gospel and working together we can be like the Lord wants us to be.

I was watching a movie the other night where this man was holding hostages in a hospital, because a doctor had done a tubulation on his wife, but only after her request. The man didn't see it that way, he only saw what he wanted too and that was that his wife couldn't have any more children. His baby daughter had died in that hospital after heart surgery. He was angry at the doctor and very bereaved. He was holding some women and babies and a man and wanted revenge. He asked for the doctor and also too talk to his wife. It took the voice of a child (his son)over the phone to make him realize what he was doing. The love for his son and the love his son showed him by talking to him, it made all the difference in the world. It made him realize he still loved.

The Savior loved us so much he gave his life that we might live. John 10: 18– Therefore doth my father love me because I lay down my life, that I might take it again, " No man taketh it from me but I lay it down of myself. I have power to lay it down and I have power to take it again." This commandment I have received of my Father. Christ came to live among us, so he can identify Himself with the interests and needs of us all.

He has the love of a parent whose child has gone wrong and the heartache he knows. If we yearn and hurt for our children, just think how much hurt we cause the Savior when we err and don't live the way we should.

We have the power of the Priesthood, the Elders Quorum, Relief Society and all the other organizations here on earth to help us grow.

We have the temples to do ordinances in to show our love for those people, (some we don't even know, but someday we will) that have gone on before us.

Our church is growing, we have new members coming in all time. Our ward has several new members. By the love of everyone pulling together and our wonderful missionaries and the spirit of our Savior we can accomplish the work we are here to do.

President Howard W. Hunter sais, "As members of the Church of Jesus Christ we seek to bring all truth together. We seek to enlarge the circle of love and understanding."

"Behold," Mormon proclaimed, "I say unto you that ye shall have hope through the atonement of Christ and the power of his resurrection, to be raised unto life eternal, and this because of your faith in him according to the promise." Mormon 7: 41.

We don't know exactly how Jesus accomplished the atonement. We only know that some how during the course of excruciating and agonizing hours in the Garden of Gethsemane and on the cross he became our Redeemer.

"Christ's agony in the garden is unfathomable by the finite mind, both as to intensity and cause,"—Elder Talmadge wrote. " He struggled and groaned under a burden such as no other being who has lived on earth might even conceive possible. In some manner , actual and terribly real though to no man incomprehensible, the Savior took upon Himself the burdens of the sins of mankind from Adam to the end of the world."

We as servants of Jesus Christ have been given so much love through him, that by his example we must show our love to others. We are not asked to do as he did, to give, not our life, but just to give our love.

Christ said, be faithful and diligent in keeping the commandments of God and I will encircle you in the arms of my love.

There are three things of eternal value. Faith, Hope, Love, and the greatest of these is love. I wonder if we really know just how much we need each others love. It is the most precious thing we have and it is free if only we open our hearts and our minds. God knows what is in our hearts and minds, so I pray that you will be with our men and women in the war and protect them and help to stop all the violence and wickedness so they may soon return home to their love ones.

CHOICES

We all have choices to make, whether we make the right ones or not is up to us. Heavenly Father gave us free agency when we came to earth. We are very fortunate to be here in America where we can have that right.

We have the Book Of Mormon and the Bible and other sources of literature and the choice to read them or not.

Sometimes our life seems such a turmoil and we think, I just don't have time to read. But Heavenly Father will help us if we only take a second and ask him to.

Sometimes it's like pedaling a bike down a hill we don't know how to stop or put on the brakes, we have forgotten, so then we have to suffer the consequences.

Did you ever feel like the wheel of your life is racing faster and faster? If so read what Jesus did during the last Sabbath day of his life. Start with Matthew, there is nothing in Matthew? Read Mark, what, what did Mark say about the way Jesus spent the Sabbath? Nothing there either? Strange what about Luke? Luke doesn't say anything either. Maybe John did, surely John mentioned the Sabbath. John doesn't either? Looks like Jesus was quiet that day. One week left to live and Jesus observed the Sabbath. He still had to teach and train the Apostles but He could take time to rest and worship, with his full agenda He still had time too, so why can't we just stop ,and think, and listen to the small voice that tells us to. Slow down and trust our Heavenly Father. He will provide enough time for everything, if we ask and trust Him. I know I have felt that way for sometime. I just pray that I can be strong enough to follow the advice that Heavenly Father has given us.

Holman Hunt painted the picture of Jesus standing at the door knocking. Beneath the painting the words were written, " Behold, I stand at the door , and knock", if any man hear my voice and open the door, I will come in to him". Holman Hunt had intentionally left out something, which I had never noticed. There was no door knob on the door. It could only be opened from the inside. Hunt's message was the same as Heavenly Father's. we have to make the choice for him to come in. Come into our hearts and live eternally.

Heavenly Father comes to us and speaks to us through the scriptures. We are all invited to come and worship together.

There are lots of different kind of invitations, birthday, wedding, anniversary, and dinner and many more, but these are only for a short while. Heavenly Father's invitation is for eternity. To know our Savior is to receive his invitation, not just hear it, not just study it, and not just acknowledge it, but accept it and live it.

He is clear in what He asks and what He offers. The choice is up to us. Those who live for this world is bad news, but those who live for the world to come, it is an encouraging promise. When we hear the voice of Jesus speak the words no more loneliness, no more tears, no more death, no more sadness and no more pain.

I felt such need to write this message for myself and for some of you. That we need to slow down and listen to the still small voice, the Savior's invitation to come unto Him and learn about Him.

D&C 34: 7-9 For behold verily, verily, I say unto you the time is soon at hand that I shall come in a cloud with power and great glory,(8)and it shall be a great day at the time of my coming, for all nations shall tremble.(9) but before that great day shall come, the sun shall be darkened, and the moon be turned into blood; and the stars shall refuse their shining, and some shall fall, and great destructions await the wicked.

The Lord is clear in what He asks and what He offers, the choice is ours. We can't control the weather, the economy or if we have blue or brown eyes. We can't even choose how people respond to us, but we can choose where we want to spend eternity. So please let's choose the right.

GREED

I know at sometime or other we have all been guilty of greed. Not intentionally , but after we read some of the scriptures, I think you will have to agree.

Greed is a universal sickness. Poverty is certainly not an antidote for it, but neither is wealth. You can find greed where ever you live-it knows no class, race, nation, or language.

Some symptoms of greed are, the love of money. Not money it's self but what we do with it and how we acquire. We must work for what we want, and know how to spend it. The Lord wants us to have nice things but not if we have to cheat or steal to get it. It reads in 1st Tim. 6:10, "the love of money is the root of all evil". We can still have money and not care more for it than we do our salvation, or the love for Heavenly Father.

Living comfortably isn't a sin, but some people doesn't really know what poverty is. It seem the more a person has the more he wants. We are never satisfied.

People often mistakenly believe that God rewards righteous living with material things. That is not what he does. But he does say if you will keep my commandments ye shall prosper in the land. Also walk in his ways that we may prosper in all that we do. Believe and live his commandments and store blessing for yourself up in heaven as well as prosper in all that you do.

There is a difference in wealth and prosperity. The Lord has promised that if we serve him, we will prosper and have sufficient for our needs. Wealth is another matter. We shouldn't expect him to make us wealthy, with so many millions that don't have enough for their daily needs.

No doubt he blesses us but in (his) way. But we must never expect more than he is willing to give. One cure of greed mentioned in the scriptures is helping the poor, (Acts 4:32), (4th Nephi 1:3) (Moses 7:18).

Another cure –Be thankful for what you have. Gratitude. " If you seek the riches which is the will of Heavenly Father to give to you, you shall be the richest of all people, for you shall have the riches of eternity".

Greed is an attitude we can change. We should be thankful that the Lord has given us the means by which we can over come it. By the sacrifice of his son Jesus Christ. A sacrifice like that is the dearest thing that a person could give, his life for ours.

GRIEF

We must try to prepare our children and our self in ways to help everyone concerned. Teach them that there will always be trials, tribulations, and pain in our lives. That is part of our growing process, part of Heavenly Father's plan.

Teach them that death is as much a part of God's plan as birth. We are never fully prepared for death or other trials, but there are certain things we can do. (First)Put your life in order with Heavenly Father's accept him as your savior and live as he would want us to. Teach our children the gospel principles, to always read the scriptures and pray. Answer any questions they have. Read and pray with them. (Second)Make preparations for your funeral expenses. Most of us don't like to talk about death but it is a part of Heavenly Father's plan. We all must die to return to him.

At the time of death of a loved one it is devastating, so if we have preparations made all of us have time to grieve, and that is something we all must do , to get control of our lives.

Be sure to make a will so your estate will be taken care of. That is another burden that our love ones that are left behind will not have to worry about.

The expression of grief is not evidence of weakness or lack of faith. It is the evidence of love and our need to go on with our lives in different directions.

Death is not the only grief that touches people. Sometimes we grief because of the hardness of our loved ones heart. We want so much for them to live better.

I Nephi ch 15: 4 and now I, Nephi, was grieved because of the hardness of their hearts, and also, because of the things which I had seen, and knew they must unvoidably come to pass because of the great wickedness of the children of men.

Nephi was told by an angel of the blessings and cursings that was to take place if all were not obedient to God. Also the Lord grieved because of our sins and hard heartness. He said a faithful man would have blessings, but he knew man sinned, so he grieved for us.

Proverbs ch: 28: 13-14 He that coverth his sins shall not prosper; but whosoever confessth and forsaketh them shall have mercy. (14) happy is the man that fearth always: but he that hardenth his heart shall fall into mischief.

The Lord has given us a way to over come that grief, if we will repent and obey him.

Divorce and the loss of respect and love from a friend who finds forgiveness a difficult gift to give is also forms of grief.

Families who struggle daily with severely handicapped children or mental illness of a friend or loved one, also suffers grief.

A quote from President Kimball, "Being human, we would expel from our lives physical pain and mental anguish and assure ourselves of continual ease and comfort, but if we were to close all doors upon sorrow and distress, we might be excluding our greatest friends and benefactors. Suffering can make saints of people as they learn patience, long suffering and self master". (Unquote).

Once there was someone that asked a question, "Of all the problems in life, which would be the hardest to face?" The person answered death, I think that would be the hardest to face. The person that asked the question said, "that's what I use to think, but you know, thanks to the Lord, death is like all other problems, we'll live through it".

Grief is not a disease. It is the hardest work we will ever have to do. It is also a process necessary to take control back into our lives. Avoiding grief will not make it go away. We have to grief to put our lives back into order. The focus of control is to acknowledge the loss , do the grief, work and redefine our roll on relationship to life. Confront the loss by admitting it, telling about it and sharing it.

There is not any person that can cry the tears for another, do the grief work for another, or solve the problems for another. Jesus did not solve the problems for those he ministered to. He simple gave them the tools by which they could solve them. Our tools are prayer, scriptures, and obedience to Him, which we must use to accomplish the work He wants done.

There are four concepts we experience in grief.

(Depression) When we don't want to accept responsibilities.

(Fight/flight syndrome) Give up the will to fight our emotions and want to flee from responsibilities.

(Surrogate suffering syndrome) the possible escape

through too much sleep, excessive work, or prescription drugs.

(Differed judgement) We are holding back, just doing the things we have to and letting others help to much. We are not taking the time to grieve. Putting off the most important part of healing.

HEALING AND NOT HEALING

WHEN WE ARE NOT HEALING

(1) When we believe we are victims. We ask our self (why me).
(2)We become dependent on therapy. Getting well would mean learning to function independently as well as serving others.
(3)The title of giver becomes our identity. Some people don't want to heal. No one stays where they are unless it is worth it to them to stay there.
(4)We resort to regressive behavior. We regress into childish behavior in order to assume less responsibilities.
(5)When we participate in activities but do not enjoy them. We become more miserable while seeing others around us enjoying life.
(6)We live to much in the future or the past.

HEALING

(1)We know we are healing when we can talk about loved ones without so much emotional pain.
(2)When we can experience the full range of human emotion once more. Feeling good about what is

happening around us.

(3)We can begin to reinvest our emotions, self confidence and certainty.

(4)Good out weighs the bad. We expect some days to be painful while others are pleasant.

(5)We carry out the routine of our daily lives.

(6)We learn from our experiences, look back and prepare our self for better times.

I grieve for all the sins that I have done, I wish I could go back and do differently, but I can say that I have forgiven myself because I know that Heavenly Father has forgiven me. So now I have to keep moving forward and hoping and praying that I don't ever make the same mistakes again. If I fall short I pray that God will help me to be stronger.

I know that the Lord will help us if we only ask him. There is wisdom in him giving us trials, and sorrow, so that we might grow stronger. He says in that poem (Footprints in the sand)–where there was only one set of prints I was carrying you. He is always near by . If there were joy and peace, and happiness, there would be no test of strength, no development of character.

The Lord wants us to grow strong and always loving and caring so that we might help others in their time of need, who also are grieving. We pray that we may always be strong in our belief in Heavenly Father and for him to help us through our grief.

TRIBULATION

I would like to start with a scripture from Mosiah 23: 10, (the Lord hears the cries of Alma), Never the less after much tribulation, the Lord did hear my cries, and did answer my prayers, and has made ne and instrument in his hands in bringing so many of you into the knowledge of his truth.) Also D&C 58:2-4, For verily I say unto you, blessed is he that keepth my commandments, whether in life or in death; and he that is faithful in tribulation, the reward of the same is greater in the kingdom of heaven.

3. Ye cannot behold with your natural eyes, for the present time the design of your god concerning those things which shall come hereafter, and the glory which shall follow after much tribulation.

4. For after much tribulation come the blessings, Wherefore the day cometh that ye shall be crowned with much glory; the hour is not yet, but is nigh at hand.

I know we all have tribulations and lots of times we grumble about them, but lets try to remember they are for our growth, to help us reach our goal that Heavenly Father has planned for us.

I would like to tell you of an experience that happened to me. I know a lot of you have heard me talk about it.

I was at the age of 22 and had three children when I became real sick. My temperature was so high my husband had to call the doctor. The doctor came to my house because I couldn't walk. Then they had to take me to the hospital. My husband got me in the car and when we got to the hospital they did a spinal tap. They said they thought I had polio, but I could go home if I would stay in bed. But as I started to get dressed I passed out . Then they did more test and said it diffidently was polio and I would have to stay in the hospital. So they started to take me to a room and I remember going down a hallway, I thought it was so dark . Then I could faintly see a light. I wanted to go home to my family but I couldn't say anything. I felt that we just kept going and never did reach the light. Then I passed out again and was in a coma or something all night. Then the next morning around 11:30 I opened my eyes and I was in this room with bars on the window, and my bed didn't have a mattress, just a board over the springs and a wool blanket over the board next to me. I can't recall if I had a sheet over me or not. I was so scared I called the nurse, because I remembered coming into the hospital the night before. When she came in I heard her put a key in the door to unlock it. I ask why I was locked in there and why there were bars on the windows, but all she said was because the nurse' station was so far away from the room. I told her I knew that wasn't why, that they thought I was losing my mind. I told her to get me out of there. So right away she got another nurse and they moved me to a regular room. Then I started getting better. They had to give me therapy and I wasn't allowed to get up, not even to go to the bathroom. I stayed about ten days and just before I came home I asked if I could go to the bathroom and they picked me up and put me in a wheel chair and took me and then came and put me back to bed. They let me go home that day but I couldn't do anything.

I had a baby at home that was only crawling, so before Eugene went to work I had him to put him in the bed with me. The doctors had told me I could walk but not lift anything. So when I would have to change him he crawled to the couch and pulled upon it.

I have only one regret now. That is that I didn't know about the true gospel of Jesus Christ so that I could have brought my kids up in the church.

But I did belong to another church and was taught to pray. I sure did a lot of that. I know Heavenly Father was watching over me to help me and so I could get better so I could care for my family. I know he had more work for me. I really believe that through my prayers He kept me from being crippled. Because all I could think of was how can I take care of my family in a wheel chair.

We all have tribulations, but they are to help make us stronger and to have more patience. There is another scripture I would like to share. Romans 5: 3-5 (3) And not only so, but we glory in tribulations also; knowing that tribulations worketh patience; (4) And patience; experience; and experience hope; (5) And hope maketh not ashamed; because the love of God is spread abroad in our hearts by the Holy Ghost which is given unto us.

In conclusion I would like to say; I really do consider it a privilege and blessing to be able to study about Heavenly Father and to go to his church, and to do as he would have us to do. To be able to do the work he has for us and the tribulations that help me grow closer to him.

I, like Job, Paul, and Joseph Smith and many more people do not consider my trials and tribulations as a punishment. I consider them more of a learning and a growth to become more Christ like.

MJW

HANDS

I would like for everyone to look at your hands, and thank Heavenly Father for them. Some of ours might be ugly, or big and some pretty to look at. We should all be thankful that we can work with them and be appreciative of the things we can do with them.

Think of all the things that you can do with your hands. They are the most difficult member of the human body to capture on canvas or form in clay. The hand is a wonder to behold. Neither age, color, size, nor shape distorts the miracle of creation.

Just think of the hands of a baby. As soon as it is born we look at them to see if all their tiny fingers are there and count them. We put our hands on theirs, our finger in their tiny hand so they can grasp it as if to hang on to us. As a child grows he reaches out to us with an expression of trust.

Song in the children's song book.

I have two little hands, folded snugly and tight.
They are tiny and weak, yet they know what is right.
During all the long hours till daylight is through,
There is plenty indeed for my two hands to do.
Kind, Father I thank thee for two little hands,
And ask thee to bless them till each understands,
That children can only be happy all day ,
When two little hands have learned to obey.

Then think of the youth's hands as a training period when busy hands learn to labor–and labor to learn.

The aged hands of a lonely woman as she speaks to her child heart to heart and wipes away their tears.

A father's hands reflects the dignity of honest labor and timeless toil.

A boy and girl as their hands are clasped for eternal marriage.

The placing of hands on our head for a blessing.

A hand for a vote of thanks for the wonderful work that is accomplished by our loved ones.

Another hand—The hand of the Lord, as He guided Moses and strengthen the hand of Joshua -the hand promised to Jacob when the Lord declared, "Fear thou not; for I am with thee; be not dismayed; for I am thy God:...I will behold thee with the right hand of my righteousness".

(Isa. 41: 10 The Lords hand that bless little children, the strong hand that opened deaf ears and restored vision to sightless eyes, cleanse the leper, healed the lame, even raised the dead Lazarus. With his fingers there were messages written in the sand which the winds did erase but honest hearts did retain..

With God's hand he knocks upon the door of our understanding. "Behold I stand at the door and knock if any man hear my voice, and open the door, I will come in to him, and sup with him, and he with me".

There are so many figurative ways in the scriptures. I can't begin to write all of the ways that we use our hands. What a wonderful member of our body. I thank Heavenly Father every day for my hands and the things he has let me do with them. I see some people without hands and think how blessed I am to have two that helps me to do the things that I can, wether it is to work or play, and to care for my children.

MARRIAGE IS A GREAT ADVENTURE

I'll start by saying I have been married fifty years. I have six wonderful daughters and had one boy whom God chose to be with him at the age of fifteen months. I can't say that everything has been good because we all have our struggles. But we all have to go through trials. I feel that is a way of life and it helps us to grow stronger and closer to our Heavenly Father.

It makes it very difficult when you are the only member that attends church. Because there is a closeness that we are missing. It helps us to be stronger when we worship together. I know my family believes in the Lord, I think it is just the worldly things that they can't give up or rather they just aren't ready to. But we are still a very close family. We always get together, not only on holidays but just anytime one of us feels like it.

I have found that since my oldest daughter was in a car accident that we are more considerate of one another.

My husband senses when I am disturbed and have so much on my mind that he always has a joke for me. That is something we didn't have when the children were small, it was as though we didn't ever have enough time. We both worked outside the home and with the housework and caring for the kids we felt we didn't have time for ourselves. But I would like to say to everyone, make time to be together even if you leave your housework, dishes, floors, beds and etc. Then you can do them together, because you never know what time one of you may be gone and then you have lost that precious time. Also the same with your children because one day they will be married and maybe not live close enough that you can visit just anytime you want to.

I know there is work that has to be done but do it together, and try to make your work fun.

My husband is quiet and slow to make friends or I should say not as outspoken as I am. He can take his time doing something, and if I see something, or want something done I want it done right then. If I get a phone call that is upsetting I will get nervous and sometimes angry, while my husband just calmly says wait a minute, stop and think is it really that bad.

There is a real strength in opposition between a man and his wife because if we work hard at loving and trying to understand one another we can accomplish what is best for each of us.

I would like to tell you a story about when I first got married. My husband was out of the army only about three months when we got married, and at that time he was very nervous. We had this old car, 1933 Plymouth, it didn't have a starter and the brake pedal wouldn't come back after you put the brakes on, so we tied a piece of an inner tube to the steering wheel, so when we put the brakes on we could pull the pedal back up.

At that time we lived in Tennessee on a big hill. I was expecting my first child. I was about five months, when we started to go some place in the car, we always had to park it on the hill facing down and when we started to leave, Eugene would have me ride on the running board (which the ones now don't have), and we would have to give it a push to start it rolling down the hill with my hand on the carburetor to pump the gas up so it would start.

Well sometimes it still didn't start. At the foot of the hill there was a creek and when it didn't start it would just roll until we were right in the middle of it. My husband would yell at me because he thought I didn't have my hand on the carburetor, and jump out of the car and throw rocks at the car. Of course I would cry and tell him not to get so upset. Then we would have to walk over to his mom's house, which was about two miles, to have his brothers to come and help us push it out of the creek.

At that time in our life my husband was the one that would get so upset. But through the years we have managed to cope with our oppositions.

My dad told me when I told him I was getting married, if I made my bed hard not to come back to him, for me just to lay on it. Well sometimes it was pretty hard but I never let my parents know if we were having problems. We would work them out ourselves.

Now we have been married fifty-six years and have fifteen grandchildren and twenty great grandchildren, and one great-great grandchild, and we are closer now than we have ever been.

MY TALK ABOUT CONVERSION

Today is very special to me, because I have someone very dear visiting with me, my brother from Atlanta, Georgia, and he came to church with me. When we were children we use to argue all time, or I should say I was the worse, because he was always the one to give in. Maybe because I was the youngest of five children.

When brother Wells ask if I would give a talk, I asked him what about. He said to tell how I was converted. I had something written but it was a while ago.

First I would like to ask the spirit to guide me, because I don't always say the things I mean to. They just don't come out the way I mean for them to.

Most of you know me, I don't know how well, but I will tell you a little about myself. I was married at the age of fifteen, had my first daughter at sixteen. Then my husband and my daughter and I came to Detroit, Michigan.

We stayed in Detroit fourteen years and my husband was laid off from the automobile factory. I was also working at General Motors, but he didn't feel right with me working and him being laid off, so we left and went to Chicago, Illinois. We both worked there for about eight months and then he was laid off again, so we came to Tecumseh, Michigan.

I have six girls and had one boy. Our boy died at the age of fifteen months with whooping cough. I have fifteen grandchildren and thirteen great grandchildren. I am thankful to Heavenly Father for all of them, but I have to admit I don't like the things they do. My husband is not a member of the Church Of Jesus Christ of Latter Day Saints, but he supports me in whatever I want to do.

Before my hands started shaking, I would always write in my journal. Sometimes I feel the need to express my thoughts so I would write the way I felt. What I'm about to read to you was written sometime ago.

Before I joined The Church of Jesus Christ of Latter Day Saints, I belonged to the Church of Christ, and then changed to the Methodist Church. I still wasn't satisfied. There just seem to be something missing. I didn't want any commitments because I just wasn't comfortable with some of the teachings. Some of the things they said in the church really hurt me and I just couldn't believe them. One preacher told me that my two oldest children was going to hell and it was my fault. They were typical teenagers . They just wasn't going to church. I knew they needed the Lord in their lives and I did also. But I tried several churches besides those two but I just couldn't believe all they taught. By then I had six children, but still couldn't make up mind where to go so I just stopped going altogether and stayed home and studied my bible everyday.

My neighbor belongs to The Church of Jesus Christ of Latter Day Saints, so she introduced my youngest daughter, Connie to the missionaries about eight months before I decided to be baptized. She took the discussions and was soon baptized. I even sat in on a couple with her but there wasn't anyway I was going to read The Book of Mormon. I even went to church with her because I wanted to see if she knew what she was doing. At the time she was nineteen but you know how mothers are. We try to protect our children.

Then one day she left her Book of Mormon on the table and it was open. I noticed the date , April 6th, so I just had to find out what that date was because my dad was born on April 6th . As I read on there was Sept 22nd . I stopped real fast and my mind flashed back to when one of my daughters was born. (I lay in the hospital thinking, there is something special about today, not just my baby's birth because I already had five children and I loved one just as much as the other. I felt closer to Heavenly Father than I ever had and I knew there was something special about that day but I didn't know what at the time).

After sitting for awhile I knew why I had felt that way. So I started reading the Book of Mormon and asked about the discussions. I started going to church again after about three months.

It was hard because I smoked about one and a half packs of cigarettes a day for almost forty years.. The missionaries discussed this with me and ask me if I believed in blessings. They explained it to me and I told them I would like to have one because I sure did want to stop smoking but felt I needed help.

One night after that I wanted a cigarette so bad , I called the missionaries on the phone and talked to them. They said they would come out. I told them no because there was a little snow on the ground and they didn't have a car. They would have to ride their bike, so I told them I would be okay. I lived about five miles from them, but in about twenty-five minutes they were knocking on my door. They were so cold that I really felt bad, and said to myself, if they cared that much to help me, I know I can quit.

I also had a blessing to help me to stop drinking coffee. I would drink as much as three or four pots a day. So I stopping smoking and drinking coffee in about ten days. That was in November 1984. Then we had a New Year's Eve dance at the chapel for our ward and I set the date for my baptism. It was January 26, 1985. Since then I have had so many blessings from my Heavenly Father, and I feel so much better and I am happier.

I guess we all have to have some incentive to do something , and mine was a result of my daughter leaving her Book Of Mormon on the table open at those dates. Please ask yourself am I getting the happiness and satisfaction that I want out of life.

At first it was very hard. I guess I was being tested. My children didn't come over as much to visit me, which was very unusual. They were always calling or coming over before. I had some disagreements with my husband, not about the church, but just trials. I know I was being challenged to see if my faith was strong enough. After a month or so everything started to get better. My children started coming back and they respected my decision. Sometime we still disagree on some things but I can feel my husband and children growing closer to Heavenly Father. I know with our prayers they will someday except the gospel.

My daughter that is a member and myself are always trying to comfort one another. The most comforting thing to know is that Heavenly Father loves us and wants each and every one of us to obey his commandments so we can live with him again someday.

I want to thank the Elders that taught, and baptized me. They were Michael Barzee, and Elder Thomas Paterson. I also thank Heavenly Father for sending them to Michigan, on their mission.

Since I have written this there have been many changes. My daughter Connie and my neighbor Nancy Caldwell have both gone inactive from the church. Which I truly regret. We still discuss things together and I know in my heart that they still believe and that someday they will come back to church.

The trials that I am going through at this time, I don't know how I could make it without the gospel in my life.

I know I was only suppose to tell you how I was converted, but my heart is so full I feel the need to say a little more.

A scripture in John Ch 14:1,(Jesus said), let not your heart be troubled; ye believe in God, believe also in me. Another scripture in D&C 50:41-42, Fear not little children, for you are mine and I have over come the world, and you are of them that my Father hath given me; and none of them that my Father hath given me shall be lost.

I feel like a little chick and Heavenly Father has taken me and is comforting me like a mother hen protects her chicks as she spreads her wings all around, He has his arms wrapped around me.

Please if you don't know what happened on April 6, 1829, and on September 22nd, read the Book of

Mormon. I have a testimony that Jesus Christ lives and he is here helping me through my ever day life.

DISCOURAGED OR DEPRESSED

"Eye has not seen, nor ear heard, things that God has prepared for them that love Him."

There is only one way to look when the day is dark and that is to look up to God, where the sun is always shining.

As the days go by and we see are lives as a whole, we realize that through the miraculous power of His love, in some way beyond our understanding, all things have worked together for good.

Often it seems to us here on the earth that our work for the Lord goes unnoticed, unappreciated and sometimes seems to be in vain. But it is not so in the eyes of the God, for the promises of the Lord are, "If any man works abide, he shall receive a reward." (1 Cor. 3:14). So through faith God turns our disappointments, unfilled dreams, heart aches and frustrations into a beautiful morning.

There are so many people in this world that are depressed. Ones that are on medication, seeing a consulor, and if they would only turn to the Lord let Him help them how much better they would be. I'm not saying that we still don't have problems because we do, but they are so much easier to bear.

The Lord said Ye who are burdened and heavy laden, come unto me and I will give you rest.

Sometimes you think things are bad but just remember it can be worse. I have had lots of problems in my life, polio. different surgeries, epilepsy, and many others, but when one of your children is sick or someone in your family that is the most depressing. I am very fortunate to have the gospel in my life and I thank Heavenly Father everyday.

If every time we get depressed we should remember our Savior, and just how much he suffered for us.

PEACE BE STILL

We have a song in our hymn book at church, that touches my heart ever time we sing it. Some of the words in it, peace be still. I just think how many times that I have felt the warmth of Jesus' arms around me, and felt that peace. Sometimes we just don't take time to feel his love, we are to busy with our own thoughts and our debts and other troubles that invade our life. We all need to stop and meditate and relax from our problems and let Jesus help us take care of them. Jesus says, "Ye who are burdened and heavy laden, come unto me and I will give you rest".

When I was working outside of the home, working eight hours a day. I had a baby sitter for the children, but she didn't do much but baby sit. I would come home to a dirty house and dirty dishes and I would have to clean house, then dishes and then fix something for the children to eat. Then I started laundry and giving baths so the could get ready for bed and at that time we ironed all of our clothes. By that time it was time for bed. So I would get my bath and then start to bed. I started to say my prayer and before I could finish I would feel the Saviors' arms around me and sometimes I never got to finish my prayer. He would give me so much peace I would forget all of my worries.

Then the next morning it was the same thing over again. But it didn't matter how hard I worked, I always thought how thankful I was to have such a wonderful family, and to know that the Lord had given them to me to care for.

When you think, I don't know if I can do anymore.

You can always manage some way . My mother-in-law was in a car accident and had a broken leg and an arm and was in bed with casts on both, she couldn't even get out of bed or even turn over by herself. I was pregnant with my fifth child but we told her she could stay with us. Yes, it was hard and I was still working at a factory, but the Lord saw us through our trials. He kept me strong so I could care for the ones that really needed me.

I know that I should have taken more time to read and play with my children but I just didn't have enough time. I still did the best that I could and I know that Heavenly Father knows that. I just pray that they will do the things that they have been taught. That they will take time to listen to the spirit and as the song says, peace be still.

As my husband and I were going to Tennessee one summer we stopped at a rest area, then when we started back to the car it started pouring rain. My husband was upset at the time and said, "Oh great I guess we will have to wait or get wet". I told him to be patient, maybe it was for the best, and sure enough it stopped in about fifteen minutes. Then we got back to the car and as we got just about fifteen minutes down the highway there was a real bad accident. If we had left in the rain we would have been right in the accident. So if we will just stop and listen to the spirit as the Lord says, " peace be still he will guide us. So be still and listen and you will have peace.

DEATH

It is the will of nature that our mortal body be laid aside when the soul is entered into real life. This is rather an embryo state– a preparation for living. A man is not completely born until he is dead. Death is a form of life which, we do not yet understand.

Someone said and I quote: " what we call death is the operation of life----what we commonly call death does not destroy the body. It only causes a separation of spirit and body."

I have learned to think of death as birth—this life and this earth as the pre-natal beginning of the everlasting life that follows. We each develop physical organs while in a mother's womb, so we develop spiritual qualities while we are here on this earth.

D&C 42: 45— Thou shall live together in love, in so much that thou shall weep for the loss of them that die.

We seem always to be nearer to God when we are having trials and tribulations, which he permits for us to have time to purify and cleanse our souls, which every person needs in our life to be able to carry on with our ever day work.

An unidentified author wrote; for tis sorrow that works our pondering, and grief that teaches us to feel.

We seem to be in shock when someone close to us dies, but there are some things that are really clear in our minds. There was this person that was telling a story at his friends service about a sailing ship, in a beautiful blue lagoon on a clear day. A fine sailing ship spreads its brilliant white canvas in a fresh morning breeze and sails out to the open sea. We watch her glide away magnificently through the deep blue and gradually see her grow smaller and smaller as she nears the horizon. Finally where the sea and the sky meet, she slips silently from sight; and someone near says. "There she is gone". Gone where? Gone from sight that is all. She is still as large in mast and hull and sail, still as able to bear her load, and we can be sure that, just as we say, "there she is gone"! another says, "there she comes".

While we are morning the loss of love ones, others are rejoicing to meet them in the spirit world. The spirit world is a place of joy and peace. It is also a place of continued progress. The spirit world is close by, though not visible to our mortal eye. We are all made of dust. In Eccl, ch 12:7 It reads, then shall the dust return to the earth as it was; and the spirit shall return to God who gave it.

The suffering and grief for someone we care for is God's way of letting us heal and to do the work He has for us here on earth, we know He stands ready to give us strength we need to endure- if we have the faith necessary to do His will. We are all here for as long as god wants. So all we have to do is obey and he will guide us to everlasting life.

It is only natural for us to morn for our loved ones. God says we are only human so that is our nature to morn for our loss, because we cannot see through the veil to know what awaits us. If we could we would be happy for our loved ones. To know that they are in a better place. Where there is no more pain and no more tears.

GOD HAS A PLAN FOR US

Before we were formed in the womb, God had a plan for us. We were spirits in the spirit world. He knew what was going to happen to all of us before we were even born. We wanted to come to earth and obtain a body just as Jesus Christ. We knew we would have trials, sorrow and pains. But in order for us to become as Jesus we would have to endure all that the Lord wanted us too, so that when we die we can go back to live with Heavenly Father. It is a very hard thing for us to do sometimes, but we have to remember all the suffering and pain Jesus went through to pay for our sins. We must pray and always be strong and the Lord will help us to get through anything he has for us to do.

We are here on earth to multiply and replenish it, yes, we have pain and sorrow and sometimes we feel that we can't take anymore, but the Lord is always nears us to help us through. He knows our strength and our weakness even better then we do and he provides a way for us to find comfort. Just by trusting Him and praying and always have faith, because He will always take care of us. Sometimes we feel He has forsaken us, but He says, " I will never leave you or forsaken you, I will never put any more on you than you can bear".

He tells us we must live by faith. We say, " what is faith"? "Faith is substance of things hoped for, the evidence of things not seen". Our faith must stand in the wisdom of God. Have confidence in things we cannot see. Sometimes things seem dark and our faith is tested but we should never lose hope. For one day we will fully see through darkness into the light. We will understand his mercy and his love. We will see no witness of it, until after the trial of our faith.

Our children do things that hurt us and also hurts our Heavenly Father. We also do things that hurt Him. But we are still God's children and our children he has given us, only for awhile, until He wants them back. So we are not responsible for what our children do after they become old enough to know what is right and what is wrong as long as we teach them right. We are not held responsible, it hurts us but it also hurts God.

Jesus went about his life healing the sick, making the blind to see, and all kinds of miracles. He invites us to cast our burdens upon him. He said, "my yoke is easy and my burden is light". Matt: 11:30. As he was nailed to the cross and was dying he cried out, "Father forgive them; for they know not what they do". Luke13:34.

Heavenly Father even had a plan for his son, Jesus Christ. Jesus carried out his plan without any criticism. His life for us so we can have eternal life.

We need not fear as long as we have the power of faith and live by God's word. Yes, God has a plan for us.

We can not comprehend all that He has for us to do. But we can learn a little at a time, " precept upon precept: line upon line; here a little and there a little". Isa 28:10.

Now as we go forward with faith , God's plan is being fulfilled. We don't know when it will be all filled, but that is His will, not ours.

It is a marvelous and wonderful thing for all of us,

who desire to know the truth, because we can receive it by the studying of God's Word. (The Scriptures) It will take prayer and seeking the truth, and living the gospel, and by the power of the Holy Ghost, we will have knowledge.

There had to be an atonement for God's plan, so it was through the sacrifice of Jesus Christ, the only sinless person here on earth, and the only one capable to correct and atone for our sins. It is through his death that God's plan is perfected for us, that we may live again after our death. "For in Adam all dies, even so in Christ shall all be made alive".1st Cor.15:22.

The atonement of Jesus Christ redeems all mankind from the fall of Adam and causes all to be answerable for their own manner of life. John 3:16-17 it reads, For God so loved the world that he gave his only begotten Son that whosoever believeth in him should not perish but have everlasting life, 17 - For God sent not his Son into the world to condemn the world; but the world through him might be saved.

So our life is all planned out by Heavenly Father. We only have to accept the things we can't change and pray for God's help to understand and give us patience to endure.

About the Author

Mary was born and raised in a small town in Tennessee. She married when she was 15. She and her husband, Eugene, had seven children. She currently lives in Tecumseh, Michigan with her husband of 57 years and enjoys spending time with her children and grandchildren.

Printed in the United States
24085LVS00001B/268-360

9 781932 852561